Self-Help for Small Business

(Beat Big Business with Value-Add)

by Pat Taylor

ISBN 978-1-463562-92-2

Printed in the United States of America.

Design by Sue Peterman

To my children,
who move me to do well

Contents

Sales Savvy:
Self-Help for Small Business

by Pat Taylor

Savvy, Not Size

There is a "brotherhood" of salespeople; a community of men and women that represents the universal opportunity to improve one's station in business and in life. Selling equals freedom — from poverty, from fear, from limitations. It is woven into the fabric of free enterprise. Selling is the key we need to unlock the American Dream.

As a former Marine, I know a thing or two about brotherhood. There is no tighter fraternity in the world than the United States Marine Corps; our esprit de corps is legendary. We hold sacred the values of honor and integrity, and place our faith in the discipline that keeps us focused and strong in times of conflict. Discipline and integrity bond Marines for the rest of our natural lives; forever, we are brothers and sisters in the Corps.

When I completed my military service, a former Marine helped me make the transition from military to business life. He showed me how the Marine Corps traditions of discipline and integrity could serve me in a professional career as a salesperson. He initiated me into a new "brotherhood." Not a fellowship of soldiers, but of salespeople — civilian defenders of our way of life. Defenders of free enterprise.

Many are the rags-to-riches stories built upon successful careers in sales. Celebrated are the tales of immigrants to our country who would sell newspapers and apples and shoe shines for the promise of independence in America. Most of these "small business owners" who worked hard made a living; some realized their dreams.

Of course, "selling" means different things to different people. It can refer to a simple transaction. It can be a synonym for "marketing." In this book, however, "selling" refers to the art of persuading a person or company to pay more for your small business's product or service than they might for a cheaper alternative from a big company. Your ability to demonstrate something different and to convince the prospect or customer that the difference is "more expensive and worth it" is paramount to your small business's long-term success.

That ability to differentiate is the gist of this book. I'm going to talk about a lot of things — sales things, some business things, even a few people things. But the one consistent theme will involve differentiating your small business to attract new clients and increase your profits. Differentiation is important to you because it is the secret to [small business] David beating mighty [big enterprise] Goliath. Just as Marines have emerged victorious over larger and more powerful foes, a small business's differentiation enables it to rise above the low-price tactics of Big Business and win the customers' business. It takes savvy, not size. All you need is insight into the value of differentiation, the ability to demonstrate — with integrity — that which makes your product or service unique, and the discipline to persist.

This is a handbook of observations, suggestions, and reminders of things that help us differentiate ourselves as small businesses, and keep us mindful of the sales techniques we use to succeed as businesspeople. How to differentiate and sell that difference for a premium is what I talk about in the pages that follow. The anecdotes and advice come from personal sales experiences.

Chapter One

The Need to Sell

"If we don't sell, we don't survive."

If we don't sell, we don't survive. Cash flow is the direct result of sales, and no business can survive without it. We can simulate cash flow with venture capital or bank loans, but sooner or later, someone has to make a sale.

This is so fundamental to business success that I feel it's almost senseless to write a chapter about it. The need to sell is universal and constant; certainly everyone knows that "the main thing is the sale." Maybe not; maybe I take it for granted that everyone knows because it was different for me. The need to sell became an important part of my life very early on ...

I like to say that I grew up in a large family: I had four mothers and two fathers, and more grandparents than I could count. When my mother divorced the second time, my siblings and I moved to Texas from California to be with our father's new family. We moved 1,250 miles, two time zones, and three steps down the economic ladder in a little less than a week.

It was made very clear to us during the first few days in our new "home" that there would be no money for college, no support of any kind for a proper education. We would be cared for through high school, but from that point on, we would have to find our own way in life. So I began to work as soon as I could find a job.

I sold newspapers in the sixth grade, but the dollar-to-hassle ratio wasn't working for me. I was up at 5 o'clock in the morning rolling and throwing papers seven days a week. I went door to door making collections, hoping to catch customers at home. For this, I made a few dollars a month. I needed to find something more lucrative.

In my second year of junior high, I found an Amway guy building a team who agreed to let me participate. For the next eight months, I went door to door selling cleaning supplies to housewives. The ladies in the neighborhood were very kind to "the boy from Martin Lane" and bought what they could from me. I didn't make a lot of money, but the repeat business added up. Moreover, I learned that if I was persistent in knocking on doors, I would unfailingly find customers for my products.

I worked retail until I graduated from high school. Then I joined the United States Marines. Toward the end of my service, while working as a recruiter (selling young men a future in my beloved Corps), I met a former Marine who showed me how our core values of discipline and integrity could be leveraged in the business world. I learned that I was no longer economically shackled by my lack of formal education. I learned that the bedrock of success in any small business is the ability to make a sale. If I was willing to work uncommonly hard and summon the courage to make the calls, I had the wherewithal to realize my dreams. This has been proven true in my life and could be equally true in yours.

Life deals everyone both good and bad hands, and like many people I've had my fair share of both. I share my past with you so you will understand that the recipes for success presented in this handbook are based not on Ivy-League concepts or business school theories, but on real-life experiences learned from an early start and a long lifetime of actually "making the sale."

I have heard of products that sell themselves, but most products have to be sold. We have to meet people (most of whom we don't yet know) and convince them to try our goods. There is a need to sell them on the features and benefits of the product (or service) and demonstrate the value in that to them. This is not an easy thing to do, and there are very few people who want the job. Believe it or not, there are salespeople who don't want to sell.

There is a need to sell the customer on the fact that our small business's premium product or service is worth more than the competition's low-priced offering. Small businesses can't compete on price with Big Business; our goods are going to cost more. Whether our higher prices are due to superior product materials and craftsmanship or a function of a superior support system, customers need to be convinced that they will get more for their money if they purchase premium goods from us.

There is a need to sell the customer on the fact that we intend to cultivate long-term relationships. They must understand that mega-retailers and superstores are not interested in any kind of relationship beyond the transactional relationship that they (as a customer) represent that day. There is a need to sell customers on the idea that small businesses treat customers better, and better treatment is more valuable than any Reward Points program a superstore offers.

There is a need to sell the customer the reality that, as a small business, we have genuine enthusiasm for customer satisfaction. We don't really have to sell that enthusiasm; it sells itself. But we must demonstrate the enthusiasm that differentiates our companies from Big Business, because that enthusiasm is contagious. A customer who shares our enthusiasm for our company's premium brand is happy to pay a higher price for our products and services. (Look at Apple product customers.) Moreover, they are happy to tell their friends and provide us with good customer referrals.

There is also a need to remember to sell. Unfortunately, one of the biggest problems we face is that we often forget to schedule this most important activity. As critical as selling is to the success of a small business, we always seem to find something else to do. Maybe we have a management meeting this morning and a lunch appointment with a vendor. Perhaps we've got to talk to the service manager about a customer complaint this afternoon. We've got so much to do that we forget to sell. It happens almost every day of every week, and before we know it, we forget to tend to that most important thing — selling.

When all the excuses are wiped away and we look at our activities and their impact on the bottom line, it comes down to this: If we don't sell, we don't survive. When we distill all of our activity down to the very essence of success, the following fundamental truths remain: A company's ability to sell its unique character and product quality is reflected in that company's profits. A company's ability to reach its sales goals is reflected in its proficiency for reaching its goals for growth and profitability. A company's ability to sell determines its ability to survive. If we don't learn to schedule time for selling and to make the best use of that sales time, our businesses are not going to survive. There is (and always will be) a never-ending need to sell.

In Summary: The Need to Sell

- If we don't sell, we don't survive.
- There is a need to sell the product or service. I've heard about products that sell themselves, but most products need to be sold.
- There is a need to sell the value of quality. People will pay more to get more, but a salesperson has to demonstrate the added features or quality that justifies the extra cost.
- There is a need to sell the benefits of working with a small business (as opposed to buying from Big Business at a lower price):
  - Superior quality — handcrafted products as opposed to those that are mass produced.
  - Superior service — small businesses need each and every customer, and that is usually reflected in the attention they give those customers.
- There is a need to make time to sell and a need to sell during that time. Company owners and sales managers tend to leave the selling to others. Instead, it should be a scheduled part of every workday.

Chapter Two

The People Who Sell

"All kinds of people sell all kinds of things."

Uncle Jimmy was my stepfather's brother. He was a physically and socially awkward man. Uncle Jimmy didn't talk a lot because most of what he said sounded like nonsense and he had grown tired of ridicule. But when I was enjoying the very early years of my life, he passed some surprisingly useful words of wisdom to me that have stayed with me all these years.

We were outside a church in Costa Mesa, California. It was a refuge for Uncle Jimmy, and he attended often. On this particular occasion, he offered to take me along. As we left the service and walked down the big lawn toward his blue Ford Fairlane, I told him that I felt a little intimidated by the dark and ominous overtones of the church. He listened to my observation, stopped on the path, turned to me and said,

"All kinds of people sell all kinds of things, boy."

Then he turned and walked to the car. I remember thinking *"what an oddball"*; I was thankful that we weren't genetically linked. As the years passed, however, the truth revealed itself. Indeed, the church was selling guilt and salvation just as schools and teachers sell education, and I smile now at my uncle's convoluted wisdom. Everyone's a salesperson (whether they realize it or not), and everyone is selling something.

One of the things I learned while serving with the Corps is that, while every Marine is a patriot, not every patriot is a Marine. There are innumerable civilians who contribute to the same cause and often help to win the war. In the same way, I've learned in my career as a salesman that, while every salesperson sells, not everything is sold by a salesperson. Many of those who sell things in a small business do not actually work in the Sales Department. Not everyone even knows they are a part of the sales process. In fact, there are some people in an organization who are adamantly opposed to the idea of playing a part in a sale. We are more profitable, however, when we learn to properly employ the underutilized sales resources in our company.

Technicians and product support personnel are a great example of underutilized sales resources. No matter the industry, they often enjoy the greatest credibility with the customers. But to a technician, the idea of leveraging his or her credibility to help make a sale — to being an Accessory to a Sale — is seen as a crime punishable by "three to five." They perceive salespeople as pushy, transparent, soulless parasites living off the effort and money of others. But, much to their chagrin, technicians are salespeople, too. They influence a prospect's or customer's opinion. They are considered by many customers to be the reputable Voice of Reason; a source of reliable information regarding the products, services, or technology in which that customer is interested. Technicians offer their opinions willingly, rarely thinking that they are actually engaging in the sales process. Without knowing it, they are, in fact, selling.

Secretaries and office managers are warehouses of customer insight and can contribute greatly to the sales process, but they often feel that selling to their customers would damage their personal relationships.

However, their daily interface with dozens of customers and vendors ties them into a network of sales-related information and events that could potentially increase their employer's sales. They know which companies are planning for upgrades or additions. They know who has the budget and which companies are competing for the job. They can get information that helps to determine where best to gain a competitive advantage. They're not directly involved in the sales process, but can be invaluable in efforts to generate quality leads and project intelligence. Occasionally unwittingly and often unwillingly, they contribute to the company making a sale.

Sadly, bosses sometimes forget that they are the very best salespeople of all. The business owner built the company through his or her ability to sell products and services with a passion that only comes from ownership. He knows the "higher-ups" at every account and has no trouble securing an appointment with almost any customer or prospect. The referrals he solicits are usually decision makers. She knows the products, the competition, and the tricks of the trade. With a simple phone call, she can get "the inside scoop." In most cases, there is no better salesperson in the company than the boss.

Then there are those who sell things for you who work outside your business. Business associates and vendors are great sources of referrals. They provide access to customers outside your spheres of influence and can smooth the bumpy road to new business. These associates include accountants, lawyers, bankers, association leaders, and members of networking groups. Vendors are one of my favorite sources of sales help. They can provide profitable introductions when motivated to "match make" on behalf of their customers. They identify good prospects for partnerships or customer relationships and provide professional introductions. Their interest in supporting you is in seeing you and your company become more successful and, consequently, a bigger part of their business revenue.

As you can see, "the people who sell" extend far beyond the

Sales Department. There are many people who contribute to the company's sales effort without direct sales compensation. Their interfaces with the customer are unique and influential. They sell things through "back door" communications. In low-key conversations with customers, they impart information that either promotes products or reinforces the organization's uncommon character or culture. These people are valuable resources to the customer. They influence or validate a customer's decision to buy. In one way or another, we all do.

In the next chapter, we discuss common and uncommon ways to motivate underutilized resources to participate in Sales.

In Summary: The People Who Sell

- All kinds of people sell all kinds of things.
- Salespeople sell, but not everything is sold by salespeople.
  Every company has underutilized sales resources who
  could contribute to the sales effort. The most common un-
  derutilized sales resources are:
  - Technicians/product support personnel: They have
    great credibility with customers, but want nothing to do
    with the business of Sales.
  - Secretaries/office staff: They have access to all kinds of
    important sales information through their contact with
    customers and vendors.
  - Managers/business owners: They are (generally) the
    best salespeople in the company, but have delegated the
    responsibility for sales to the Sales Department and no
    longer participate in the effort.
  - The company's business associates: They can be valu-
    able resources for leads and introductions. Company
    lawyers, bankers, and accountants can provide useful
    third-party referrals.
  - Vendors/suppliers: They are ideal "matchmakers"; they
    know everyone in the industry and can provide power-
    ful introductions.
- If a company can harness all the people who might sell
  for an organization, sales will increase dramatically.
  Since selling is not their primary responsibility, however, they will need different and unique incentives to
  motivate them to participate in the sales effort.

Chapter Three

The Motivation to Sell

"No one likes to sell."

I've heard sales managers and company owners say that everyone should be motivated by their paychecks to do whatever is necessary for the company's success. They will say that commission should be motivation enough for an individual to go out and make the sale. Sadly, I've seen those same managers and company owners neglect the important work of sales themselves by passing the responsibility for sales off to others, knowing that their sales leadership is critical to sales success. Why? Let's start by being honest and acknowledging the real problem that lurks in everyone's subconscious:

- No one likes to sell — not even managers and owners.
- We don't want to be "sold," and we don't like salespeople.
- We don't want to be like salespeople.
- We don't want to sell.

This is the real problem, because in order to realize the best chance for success, everyone needs to sell. Every customer-facing manager and employee is a potential sales resource. But they don't want to sell:

Technicians can open and close a sale, but consider Sales a white-collar crime.

Secretaries have all the inside information on customers, including upcoming bids, competition, and getting introductions. But customers are their personal relationships, and the secretary is uncomfortable "talking business with them."

The Boss is the best salesperson in the company; he built the company by building the customer base. Now he has salespeople to do the selling. The Boss doesn't sell anymore because he "hired people to do it." He would rather hire more sales reps than do it himself.

If a company can harness these resources, sales will skyrocket. But each of these resources will resist.

We need to start by emotionally and intellectually accepting the fact that the resistance to selling and being sold is instinctive and almost universal. When selling, we fear rejection, and since we feel rejected when a customer or prospect says "No," we don't want to participate in that activity. We all have a natural aversion to Sales. There are those who say they like it, but it's only because they know that the discomfort and anxiety that accompany the selling effort is natural and is, in fact, the price paid for success. They are willing to pay that price for success. They have learned that rejection isn't personal; it's just the prospect's natural aversion to a sales effort being pointed in his or her direction. Even salespeople share the aversion to being sold!

To illustrate, an anecdote:

I was invited to a social event and the girl I was dating told me that I needed to put my black slacks in the closet and wear something more "earthy." I wasn't sure what the term "earthy" meant; I assumed my girlfriend wanted me to wear something brown or green. The only thing green that I had ever worn was my Marine Corps uniform, and I wasn't wearing that to the party. So I went to the mall to buy a pair of brown trousers. Specifically, I wanted the kind with pleats in the front and, being single, I wanted them to be permanent press (or "wrinkle free"). I walked into the mall and headed for the escalator to go into the department store. The men's department was to the left, and as I walked toward it, I could see a sales guy out of the corner of my eye. You know the guy I'm talking about, that "weird sales guy." He calculated a beeline to me, and I grew more uncomfortable as he approached. He extended

an icky *"like we're friends"* handshake and asked,
"Can I help you with anything, sir?"
And I replied,

"No thanks. I'm just looking."

I'm sure you've said the same thing. It was instinctive. And it was a lie. I wasn't "just looking"; I was looking for something specific and would probably need a salesperson's help to find it. Instead, I pushed away from that weird sales guy and struck out on my own.

A half-hour later, I was in the dressing room with three pairs of trousers. I didn't know that different manufacturers made differently fitting pants. I learned that from my sales guy (the one who was "the weird sales guy" 30 minutes ago) and he was asking me more questions. I told him about the social event. I told him about my difficulty with shopping for earthy-colored clothing and that I wasn't sure if I had anything that would go with brown trousers. By the time I left, I had brown trousers, two ties, a shirt, and a new pair of brown shoes. I was as "earthy" as Johnny Appleseed. All this happened because my sales guy got through those first five awkward minutes.

It's only the first five minutes ...

The problem, I've determined, is the awkward introduction. It initiates a reaction, an instinctive human aversion to "being sold." If a salesperson can get through that awkward introduction, he or she earns a chance to make a sale.

My sales guy (the one who sold me the slacks) made the sale because he worked through the first five minutes. He didn't let my initial reaction deter him; he knew that it wasn't personal. Five minutes is about how long it takes to overcome the stereotype of a salesperson. Many people don't like to sell because they don't want to be that annoying salesperson. And this is true about salespeople at every level of an organization. We don't want to be seen as that weird sales guy. But, in the words of William Shakespeare, this is much ado about nothing.

Lawrence was an old man whom I worked with in the oilfields of Louisiana. He had a funny way of talking but was always worth a listen. Lawrence told me something once that I have used many times to overcome my resistance to selling — my fear of rejection. He said,

"Son, when you're 20 years old, you're all wound up 'bout what people think of ya. When ya get to 40, ya don't give a damn what they think anymore. But it's not 'til you're 60 that ya realize folks don't think of ya much at all."

If you're worried about what that prospect is going to think of you making a sales call, remember what ol' Lawrence said. If the call goes well, you win a new customer. But if the prospect rejects your advance, it's nothing personal. That prospect will forget all about you before he gets up to go to lunch.

Even when armed with this knowledge — that the stereotype we fear can be overcome in a matter of minutes — we need some motivation to brave the difficulties of sales. Most business-people think that money is the great motivator for salespeople. I agree; selling is the universal opportunity to improve one's financial standing in life. People accept the challenges of a sales position in order to earn an above-average wage. There is profit in every worthwhile sale, and salespeople work for a share of that profit. That is why commissions are the standard method for motivating salespeople. But money is not the only thing that motivates people to sell.

People will do things for freedom
that they will not do for money.

People value autonomy. People want the ability to set their own working hours and to create and maintain their own schedules. They want to be treated like responsible adults, and are expected to act and work like adults.

This knowledge is especially useful when trying to leverage the capabilities of those not normally involved in the sales effort, like technicians and support people in purchasing and office management. Combine the traditional motivation (some sort of sales commission) with attractive portions of autonomy and creative control to get the attention of these underutilized sales resources.

If people are fearful of making sales calls (and, generally speaking, they are), then motivate them to brave rejection by dangling the carrot they find most tasty. Since the call is the difficult part of the process, reward them for every qualified call they make, and increase the reward when it's turned into a sale. Add another carrot if that contact is mined for additional qualified prospects. It isn't always money; I had a technician once who wanted Fridays off. We struck a deal that he would get a Friday off for every $10,000 worth of computers that he sold. It wasn't long before he was taking at least one paid Friday every month to be at home with his family.

Another way to overcome your team's resistance to selling is by motivating them with insight. Start by sharing clear objectives with the participants. If the team includes technicians and office support personnel, be willing to share "the Big Picture." Share the company's revenues and profit margin goal. Show them how revenues and profit margins affect their paychecks. Help them understand the part they play and the extent of their responsibilities. Support them with knowledge of their position and potential, and solicit feedback. Support them with your time and an open mind. Suggest bonus plans built on sharing profits generated by new sales. Listen to their ideas for a better way to do things. Try to remember what General George Patton used to say:

"Never tell people how to do things.
Tell them what to do and they will
surprise you with their ingenuity."

Support participants with predictable compensation plans. Whether you distribute a percentage of profits to a pool for all participating parties or have individual plans that reward departmental contributions, support them with financial opportunity that is predictably and consistently delivered.

As my Grandma Elsie used to say, "You've got to give to get."

Motivate your team to overcome their sales resistance by setting realistic goals. Not those Macho Management goals that sound like NASA planning a walk on Mars, but something believable. Set goals that are digestible. Telling your team that you want to increase sales $2 million this year may be realistic for a company doing $10 million annually, but it may prove paralyzing to a company that has never seen annual revenues at $2 million before. Sometimes it helps to break the goal down into smaller objectives; $500k a quarter sounds less intimidating than "$2 million this year." Better yet, make the objectives activity related, such as harvesting a certain number of qualified referrals every month. This ensures that both sales and prospecting efforts are getting equal attention. The best part of activity-related goals is that the sales effort is consistent in spite of the natural ebb and flow of revenue.

In Chapter Nine, I'll provide specifics on organizing departments and creating compensation plans to motivate your team to work together to sell. What I want to get across in this chapter is that we as owners and managers cannot expect to get more without giving more. We have to understand the natural and universal fear of selling that keeps our people from contributing more to the company's success. We have to address those fears and create plans that motivate our underutilized sales resources to participate in the sales effort. Our motivation for making this effort is obvious: to maximize utilization of company sales resources and thereby maximize sales.

By acknowledging and addressing everyone's natural resistance to sales and providing the motivation necessary to overcome that resistance, you differentiate your company from many of your competitors. While not obvious to your customers, the synergy of the sales staff with technicians and office support is acknowledged by the customers (consciously or subconsciously) and it does influence their buying decisions. The unified sales effort is reflected in the cross-departmental flow of sales-related information that, in the past, would have been perceived as casual conversation between purchasing and a vendor, or a technician and a customer. Because a customer is shared and cared for across the organization, everyone seems to know them and the customer feels the love. It is at this point in the relationship that the customer no longer needs to be sold; he will buy what he needs from your company as long as it is possible.

To sell effectively, your team must first know that they are selling. They must emotionally accept the fact that nothing happens until a sale is made, and that making the sale is everyone's responsibility. They must understand that everyone feels a natural resistance to sales, but that it usually dissipates in the first few minutes. Not everyone will be motivated to overcome their resistance to selling with the promise of sales commission. Some will be motivated by freedom to be creative or to exercise autonomy over their daily schedule. And when you — the business owner or manager — can differentiate yourself from the competition with the motivating compensation and support programs you put into place, you will benefit from new and powerful facets of your team's ability to sell your company, products, and services.

In Summary: The Motivation to Sell

- To be honest, no one likes to sell. There is a natural human aversion to "being sold," and each of us fears being seen as that annoying salesperson.
- Knowledge can help overcome the aversion to sales:
  - We know that our aversion to "being sold" is universal and instinctive. Everyone feels it.
  - We know that it only lasts for the first few minutes of the first meeting.
  - We know that people forget about the meeting if they decide not to buy, and that there is no lingering memory of our sales-related intrusion. We're not subhuman, just salespeople.
- People can be motivated to sell, but different people need different motivation.
  - Money (commission) is a motivator and the most common reward.
  - Autonomy is a motivator. People will do things for freedom that they will not do for money.
  - Money, autonomy, and other creative rewards can motivate non-traditional participants in the sales effort (technicians and support people, office staff, management personnel). Time off or prizes awarded for winners of sales contests or campaigns are examples of incentives.
- Set clear, achievable goals and tie rewards to the goals.
- Give people leeway in how they go about achieving those goals. If you tell people where to go, but not how to get there, you will be amazed at the results.
- Maximizing utilization of sales resources will help you maximize sales. Finding ways to motivate your entire team will prove to you the maxim, "The whole is greater than the sum of its parts."

Chapter Four

Prospecting for Gold

*"Ya gotta move a lot of material
if ya wanna find some gold."*

Prospecting is crucial to the growth of a small business. However, nothing is as intimidating or as actively ignored as prospecting for new customers. One of the most distasteful realities of small business success is found in the following words: If you want to grow your company, you have to find and meet people who you don't already know and talk to them about your products. Prospecting is the process of finding people you don't already know who will agree to an introductory sales meeting.

Being sales prospectors, my business partner and I wanted to learn what real prospecting was like, so we became card-carrying members of the Gold Prospectors Association of America. Every year from 2001 to 2005, we scheduled a summer trip to Alaska to do a little prospecting at the Cripple River Mining Camp on the coast of the Bering Sea. We would set up our sluice boxes a few dozen yards from the shoreline and dig down into the beach. We would scrape off the top layers of sand and gravel (called "material" in prospecting vernacular) and scoop up the gold-bearing black sands for our sluices. After all the shoveling and scooping and sluicing of the sands, we would collect our gold out of the riffled rubber mats that lined the bottom of the prospecting apparatus.

One day on the beach, I was totally immersed in slowly and evenly sprinkling my sands into the sluice. The wind camouflaged what seemed to be laughter; I didn't know if it was real or my imagination. I lifted my head up out of my work to look around and spotted an old sourdough with one hand on a hip and the other on a shovel. He was looking right at me with a comportment that was equal parts amusement and scorn. When we made eye contact, he pushed his hat back and chuckled as he shook his head.

"Something strike you as funny, ol' fella?" I asked.

"Yeah," he said, laughing. "You do. All bent over that box like you're lookin' for a miracle."

"I'm prospecting," I assured him.

"That's not prospecting, son. Prospecting is work. Scoopin' a spoonful of dirt every now and then ain't gonna get it done. Ya gotta move a lot of material if ya wanna find some gold."

Those words were nothing short of an epiphany to me. Sales prospecting is more like prospecting for gold than I had ever imagined. When gold prospecting, you have to shovel a lot of dirt if you want to find the gold. When sales prospecting, you have to meet a lot of prospects if you want to find a customer. I now refer to the ratio of calls to sales as the "shovel-to-nugget ratio," the quantitative relationship of prospecting calls to results. How many shovels of material does it take to find a good-sized nugget? How many calls does it take to make a good-sized sale?

Sales prospecting is hard work and fraught with negativity. Being successful in sales prospecting is a little bit like being a successful big league hitter in baseball. Hitting .300 makes you a superstar, but it means missing on seven out of 10 opportunities. Even if you're a superstar salesperson, you're going to strike out many times for every hit you get. Sales prospecting requires a strong belief in the Law of Large Numbers. (In probability theory, the Law of Large Numbers says that the average of the results obtained from a large number of trials should be close to the expected value, and will tend to become closer as more trials are performed. In other words, prospecting results only become predictable after you make a large number of prospecting calls, and the results become more predictable as the number of calls increase.) It also requires some serious self-discipline to work the numbers to your advantage.

One of the greatest sales prospectors I've ever known is the former Marine I mentioned in the introduction of this book. Lance Corporal David Burkhardt was a "point man" in a Marine Corps Recon platoon in Vietnam. Some of his noteworthy service activity is chronicled in Never Without Heroes *by Lawrence C. Vetter, Jr. After his Vietnam experience, the simple discomfort of sales prospecting was laughable to this hardened veteran. I had the good fortune of training with Burkhardt during the formative years of my sales career at a life insurance company.*

All of my prospects were "cold" in the beginning. I had sold nothing and knew no one, so I was left with no choice but cold calling prospects for life insurance sales. Burkhardt would deposit me on the front steps of the Tarrant County Courthouse in Fort Worth every Friday afternoon. My job was to scour the warranty deeds filed that week and gather as much contact information as I could about each home buyer. These home buyers were prospects for life insurance. Burkhardt wanted me to find 100 prospects before I could leave the courthouse.

Burkhardt's plan for me was to call each of these prospects on Monday. His logic was that most people would be home to accept a call on Monday night and I would ask them for an appointment to talk about the life insurance they needed to cover their new mortgage. I would make 100 calls every week. On average, five people would grant the appointment and two of them would buy. My shovel-to-nugget ratio was 100-to-2.

The actual sales numbers varied from week to week, but the basic ratio proved reliable (as dictated by the Law of Large Num-

*bers). I needed two sales a week to qualify for the national con-
vention. Knowing my shovel-to-nugget ratio, I calculated that 100
calls a week was all that was needed to reach my goal. I never
missed a week and, as a result, became the youngest salesman
ever to qualify for the company's national event.*

I didn't like spending Friday afternoons at the courthouse. I
didn't like making 100 "cold calls" every week. No one does, and
making those calls "every now and then" would have left me
short of my goal. But I made it a habit to do the things I didn't
like to do — that no one likes to do — and I reached my objective. Determine your shovel-to-nugget ratio and make a habit
of doing those things that no one likes to do. You will be well on
your way to realizing your sales objectives, too.

Emotional Barriers to Sales Prospecting

The impact of our emotions on our sales work is sometimes
overlooked. The fear of rejection and the fear of failure are emotional obstacles to a salesperson's success. They have a debilitat-
ing effect on some salespeople, almost paralyzing them in their
efforts to prospect for new customers. The prospecting aspect
of sales exposes a salesperson to more rejection than other aspects of the sales process. When a prospect rejects your request
for an appointment, it feels more personal than if he or she rejects your sales proposal (which may be due to the product or
price). When a salesperson takes that rejection personally, the
emotional impact can be difficult to overcome. The specter of
rejection casts an emotional pall on salespeople; they can become paralyzed with fear and avoid making the calls they need
to make.

One technique to deal with this emotional obstacle is to make
rejection the goal. Find a method for rewarding the effort that
results in rejection. A friend once shared a story with me about
setting a daily goal for rejected calls. He established a reward for

making the hard calls — the rejections. His shovel-to-nugget ratio was 5-to-1 and he needed two nuggets each day, so his daily goal was to contact 10 qualified prospects who declined his invitation to meet over lunch. He convinced himself that getting "10 No's" was good. In the course of making those calls, he would get the two appointments he needed to reach his sales objective.

The next time you get the big "No thanks," just remember that it's not you they're rejecting. Prospects who refuse you are just strangers who have no idea that you're a nice guy (or gal) and do not know that your product is wonderful. So straighten up those shoulders and move on to the next name on your prospecting list. You're going to hear "No" more often than not; don't let it get to you.

Another emotional obstacle to selling well is the fear of failure. The fear of failure is so commonplace that it even has its own name: atychiphobia. It is also known as "performance anxiety." The fear of failing to perform (at work, home, or play) can cause one to avoid an activity altogether. It follows that the fear of failure to sell can cause a salesperson to avoid prospecting or making the calls necessary to sell. It actually becomes a form of self-sabotage. In clinical terms, it is an avoidance behavior.

There are many ways of treating atychiphobia. One is to emotionally accept the fact that failure is the foundation of success. And since you're bound to fail from time to time in the pursuit of your goal, you might as well get used to it. It's like the baseball player who fails to get a hit seven out of 10 times, but ends up with a .300 average and that makes him a superstar.

There are many who counter their fear with self-help or motivational techniques. People buy motivational tips and techniques because they can actually make a difference. In my experience, the only way to get rid of a bad habit is to replace it with a good one. With motivational materials, we can replace the negative fear of failure with the positive expectation of success. It works, but it can take time to find the motivator that works best for you.

Here's an example of a great takeaway I found in a motivational book. The author suggested that the salesperson treat his fear of failure by breaking down the fear into manageable issues. If you're fearful of making sales calls, start out by practicing the things that lead up to a sales call. Take small steps: Instead of diving into a call on your own, sit with a mentor at lunch meetings with his customers. Instead of prospecting by making cold calls (the most difficult prospecting technique of all), practice prospecting by calling existing customers and asking for referrals — always moving a step at a time to the next fearful step. The key is to keep the fear at arm's length and out of your sight so that it doesn't paralyze you.

Another way to deal with the fear of failure is by modifying the way you choose to view failure. Instead of seeing the lost prospect or unproductive call as a failure, view it as feedback. Try to avoid interpreting the mistakes as permanent or personal. Rather, see them as pieces of your success puzzle; they are valuable pieces of experience and information that will lead you to the prize. Review the call and identify mistakes, modify your approach, and highlight good material to retain for future use.

In almost every situation, the best prescription for the fear of rejection and failure is action. These emotional obstacles to sales success immobilize us. Take action to overcome them. I remind myself to act with a screensaver that says, "Be brave and strong, and do good things"; take action (brave) persistently (strong) and increase sales (doing good things).

Prospecting Technique

Mistakenly, salespeople equate prospecting with cold calling, and nobody likes to cold call. There is no other prospecting technique as fraught with rejection. The shovel-to-nugget ratio is very low. There are better ways to prospect for new customers.

"Warm" referrals are the best prospects. To find them, it is best to begin by making a list of your spheres of influence. I know; it sounds like consultant-speak, but please bear with me.

Kenny Kremm hires prospective salespeople based upon their spheres of influence. When I was training with him, Kremm drew a diagram on a piece of paper with my name in the corner and arrows pointing to four circles. In one of the circles he wrote, "Immediate friends and family."

"This is a sphere of influence, Taylor. You have influence within this sphere of people. You can go to these people to prospect for sales as well as ask for referrals. Who else?"

He put the point of his pen over the next circle, or sphere of influence.

I said, "Work?"

He scowled as he reminded me, "You work for a computer company, moron. No one here is going to buy their computers from you. Try again."

Before we finished the exercise, we identified three additional spheres of influence: my church, a men's basketball league, and my class reunion contacts. For the next two days, I organized a list of people in each sphere of influence and placed them in my prospecting schedule. I started off this new career using nothing more than these four spheres of influence. Every person (and every business) has spheres of influence that can be mined for prospects. The most important source for new business prospects is your base of existing customers.

The amount of time we spend calling prospects to secure appointments is a function of the quality of the names we call. If we cold call people to find prospects for our products, the ratio of calls to appointments will be very high. The best way to meet prospects for your specialized product or service is through a referral, an introduction by a common friend. We will make fewer calls to secure more productive appointments if we solicit referrals and quality introductions from happy customers to use during our prospecting calls.

Through the years I've noticed that many salespeople get stuck at this point in the process. Instinctively, they know that referrals will generate better appointments than cold calling. But they all seem to respond with the same rebuttal:

"Yes, I asked my customers to give me referrals, but very few of them knew people who are about to buy [whatever it is you're selling]."

Customers resist because they feel pressured when you ask for referrals. It's uncomfortable for them. To successfully solicit referrals, you have to relieve the pressure. You have to make it easier on the customer. Let me share with you my favorite approach:

I used to own a technology company that built computers and data storage systems. Every time I asked a happy customer for referrals, he would tell me that he didn't know anyone who was about to buy a computer or storage system. So I stopped asking for the names of people who were about to buy computers or storage systems. I started asking for the names of people who use computers and storage systems. It's a very subtle change in phrasing, but the effect it has on the customer is striking. As a result of using this revised wording, I obtained many more quality names and introductions.

Additionally, the same approach made my prospecting calls more productive.

"Well, I'm not really in the market for a new computer system right now," the prospect might say. "Thank you very much."

"Yes sir, I understand that," I would reply. "But I know that when people like you and [name of customer that provided the referral] buy computers, they like to buy from people they know and trust and from reputable companies like mine. I just want to set up a meeting with you so that — down the road — when you're ready to buy computers, I'll be the guy you know. Would you like to meet over lunch, or is meeting at your office better?"

Now the prospect doesn't feel the pressure that comes with being asked for a sale; your request is very reasonable and, when supported by the reference (a trusted friend), it is a request that is easy to accommodate. This technique can be used regardless of the product or service you're selling.

So now that you know where to look for prospects and how to solicit the names of quality referrals, let's build a simple schedule that will take us from gathering names to meeting people.

Prospecting Schedule

The fundamentals of sales success are reflected in the prospecting schedule I am sharing with you now. I've used it to reach my sales goals for many years. There's nothing magical or mysterious about it, but using it consistently guarantees success.

There are five days in the average workweek. Monday is a bad day to prospect; our prospects are busy with the start of their workweek and have little time to entertain salespeople. Friday is a bad prospecting day, as most of our prospects are winding down and getting ready for the weekend. That leaves us with Tuesday, Wednesday, and Thursday for prospecting, and it is my practice to start each of these days with prospecting calls. I like to make my calls first thing in the morning before my prospects get busy with their day. The purpose of my call is to schedule an appointment for the following week and I make as many calls as necessary to meet my appointment quota.

For the sake of conversation, my appointment quota shall be two appointments per day, six appointments per week. That equates to approximately 24 appointments per month, which means I'll meet almost 300 new prospects per year. Very few of us are getting in front of that many people or creating that many opportunities to sell. Breaking the numbers down, it means that I need to schedule two appointments on Tuesday, two appointments on Wednesday, and two appointments on Thursday. These are numbers that everyone can achieve.

On Tuesday morning I make as many calls as necessary to

schedule two appointments for the following Tuesday afternoon. It may take one hour. It may take four hours. But the amount of time I spend is irrelevant; I must schedule two appointments for the following Tuesday afternoon. Wednesday morning, I repeat that process; I make as many calls Wednesday morning as is necessary to book two appointments with new prospects for the following Wednesday afternoon. I repeat the process on Thursday, making as many calls as necessary on Thursday morning to schedule two appointments for the following Thursday afternoon.

On Friday, I wrap up the loose ends from the six appointments I had that week. On Monday, I do the research that's necessary to maximize the opportunities I have with prospects in the upcoming week. And the process is repeated; Tuesday, Wednesday, and Thursday mornings are spent prospecting for appointments for the following week. And I must finish my prospecting by midday because I have appointments scheduled from the previous week for those three afternoons!

In the eyes of some salespeople, the simplicity of this prospecting schedule somehow seems to diminish its importance. But the consistent application of these basic fundamentals will result in six qualified appointments with new prospects for each week of the year. Change the appointment quota to meet your own needs. Without exception, those who have consistently used my schedule during their workweeks — regardless of their product or service — have met dozens if not hundreds of new prospects and closed business they would not otherwise have closed. And that, my friends, is the crux of the prospecting effort. Grow your account base. Grow your business.

In Summary: Prospecting for Gold

- Success comes from making a habit of doing the things that no one likes to do, and no one likes to prospect. So make it a habit!

- Remember the lesson I learned from that ol' sourdough in Alaska: You've got to move a lot of material if you want to find some gold. It is as true when prospecting for sales as it is when prospecting for gold. Find your shovel-to-nugget ratio to make a science of your prospecting effort. Leverage the Law of Large Numbers to realize your sales objectives.

- Understand that there are emotional barriers to prospecting and find the best technique for overcoming your fear of failure or rejection. This is where self-discipline becomes a critical component of your personal success in sales.

  - Understand that the prospect is not rejecting you as a person.

  - Make rejection the goal. Knowing your shovel-to-nugget ratio, work to get the number of rejections required to win a deal.

  - Understand that failure is the foundation of success. No one ever learned to walk without bouncing off their butt a few times. No one ever learned to ski without falling down a few times. Failure is the price we pay for success.

  - Take it a step at a time. View failure as feedback and modify your technique to realize success.

- Continually work to identify and mine your personal spheres of influence. Identify those social and professional groups where you have influence and go to them for sales or referrals.

- Soliciting referrals is the most effective prospecting technique. Remember that soliciting for referrals puts pressure on your customer. You can reduce that pressure and get better referrals by carefully wording your request. For example: Don't ask for the names of people about to buy your product, but ask for the names of people who use your [kind of] product.
- Use my prospecting schedule to guarantee success. Schedule time for prospecting and be disciplined about sticking to your schedule. Nothing happens until a sale is made, and few sales are made without prospecting. Give it the priority it deserves.

Chapter Five

The Art of Listening

"Ya gotta give to get."

T he worst thing a salesperson can do upon arriving for an appointment with a prospect is to start talking about himself, boring the prospect with unsolicited information about his company, its history, and its products and services. The customer doesn't want to hear it. He doesn't care. He has a business problem to solve (which is why he accepted your request for an appointment). The only time he wants to listen to you is when there is something of value to be gained by listening. Until you've listened to the customer long enough to learn about his problems, you probably won't have too much of value to say. The most common mistake made by salespeople is made when they talk too much.

On your first call to a new account, do the listening — not the talking. The salesperson who listens to a prospect will learn what that prospect values and about the problems she needs solved. By delivering that value and solution, you could win a new customer. Listening is an acquired skill and, without exception, the best listeners are the best salespeople.

Listening does all the talking.

When I was a senior in high school, I had a crush on a girl named Marissa McTildee. It was one of those sledgehammer, mind-numbing crushes that renders one speechless (which, considering my "twitterpated" state of mind at the time, was probably a very good thing). In spite of my fear of rejection, I asked her out on a date. She turned me down the first few times, but just after football season (during the ebb tide of the high school dating activity) she accepted. She accepted!

I took her to the Spaghetti Warehouse and, like a true Southern gentleman, I helped her take her seat. The waiter came and I said,

"Two glasses of iced tea, please."

For all practical purposes, that was the last thing I said all night. Marissa talked about school and her friends and the drill team. She talked a lot about the drill team. She talked about her family, her mom and dad, and her little brother. When she slowed down, I would prime her with another question. Marissa talked until I pulled up in her driveway and walked her to the door.

Then, unexpectedly, Marissa McTildee took my face in her hands and planted a great big smooch on my kisser. When she let go, she smiled and asked,

"Want to do the same thing next week?"

I was flabbergasted! A one-two punch delivering a knockout. A kiss — from Marissa McTildee — and another date? I wondered what might have caused something this strange and wonderful to happen. Could it be my good looks? Not likely; I was one of those guys who reminded girls of their brothers. Maybe my engaging personality? No sir, I don't think so. It couldn't have been anything I said, because I was listening all night.

"Wait a minute," I thought. "I was listening all night! That was it!"

That was the secret to gaining Marissa's attention. I listened and she appreciated it. And, as luck would have it, I held her attention by listening for many months to follow ...

Listening gets results; it makes the prospect comfortable with you and arms you with information. But it's important to qualify the type of listening to do on a sales call. With passive listening, very few questions are asked and there is no effort to steer the prospect into a particular business opportunity. It generally revolves around the customer's business history and personal interests. Active listening involves asking insightful questions to direct the conversation while gathering specific types of information. With active listening, you reenergize and direct the conversation with questions. You learn to ask questions that lead to the next round of listening. Be brief; the customer's hearing is selective. Ask his opinion; most people will give one willingly. Here are a couple of examples of questions that you can use to steer a conversation during the initial sales call:

"Tell me, please, how you started your company."

"Did you build this business to fulfill a passion or to meet an opportunity?"

"Do you remember 'the good ol' days,' or are they yet to come? What are your plans?"

"Help me understand why you think that X is a better fit for you than Y."

With active listening, we ask questions and then we listen. We don't take notes while we're listening or otherwise divert our attention; we maintain eye contact with the individual and give him both ears. We respond to pauses with follow-up questions that are the result of actively listening while he answered the previous question. This does more than provide you with all the information you need to make a sale; it bonds you to the prospect. It is very likely that you will be the only person who actively listens to that person for the rest of the day, and it has a powerful affect on the individual. It works to calm and persuade even the most hostile prospects.

I was in Chicago working with one of our local resellers. One of my favorite sales guys picked me up outside the O'Hare airport. Priding myself on my powers of observation, I could sense from his demeanor that this day was going to be different before I even got into his car.

"Where are we going today, Tom?" I asked.

"We're going to see Rodney," he replied. He wasn't looking at me and struggled to maintain a straight face.

"Rodney?"

"Yeah, Rodney the UNIX guy. Remember him?" Tom glanced over at me with a smirk on his face. "He's going to hate you, man." And he chuckled as he shook his head and turned out onto the freeway.

I had about a half-hour to consider the meeting between Rodney the UNIX zealot and Pat the Windows advocate. From a technical perspective, we were polar opposites. Windows was a relatively new computer operating system that suffered from a reputation of being unreliable. UNIX was a very mature, very stable computer operating system. UNIX nerds mastered terms like "gre" and "tar" (instead of "search" or "backup") and became computer prima donnas. There's an old joke that says, "If you have trouble sounding condescending, find a UNIX user to show you how it's done." It's not too far from the truth.

Rodney's reputation preceded him. According to the sales team, he fit the description of a UNIX administrator perfectly. He hated Bill Gates. He questioned the stability of the Windows platform. He was, in fact, "Windows hostile." When we walked into the building and sat down at the conference table, I offered my name and little else. Instead, I asked,

"Rodney, would you tell me a little about your UNIX background? Where did you first get involved with it?"

So began our relationship. Rodney talked about joining the United States Navy. About his training and experience. He shared some anecdotes about his service life, and I mentioned my experience with the Navy while serving as a United States Marine. Then I asked him about Windows.

"It's unstable. Its bloated code and it 'blue screens' every other day. I can't put it into this environment. We're mission-critical here."

I asked him to tell me more about his current mission-critical system. He was happy to do so …

After he talked himself out, I reminded him of how few workflows ran on UNIX anymore. I agreed that it was a shame, but Windows was taking over the printing workflow marketplace. Then I asked the "yes/yes" question:

"Since migrating to Windows is inevitable, Rodney, would you rather do it now or wait until next year?"

By the end of the meeting, Rodney felt like he had a new friend who understood and shared his concerns. A technology friend who understood the mission- critical nature of his business. A partner to rely on who would walk him through the transition to Windows. I left Rodney's office with a handshake and, three days later, I had a purchase order for $85,000.

I didn't talk Rodney into buying a Windows infrastructure; I "listened" him into it. I asked four questions during an hour-long meeting and listened the rest of the time. Rodney is a happy customer today because we delivered a product that met his needs, and we knew how to build that product because we took the time to listen to all of his concerns.

In Summary: The Art of Listening

- Prospects don't want to hear you talk; they want to hear you "listen."
- Know the difference between passive listening and active listening. Passive listening is letting the prospect steer the conversation. If she asks questions, answer succinctly. Resist the temptation to commandeer the conversation the first time the prospect asks you a question. This is not the time to make the sale.
- Making the sale happens after you have engaged the prospect with active listening, asking questions that steer the conversation, culminating in yes/yes questions (addressed in more detail in Chapter Seven). This engagement builds a bond with you and the prospect.
- Prospects will tell you everything you need to know to make the sale, if only you will listen. Refrain from taking notes; concentrate on the prospect. Maintain eye contact and reenergize the conversation with questions that lead to your desired outcome.

Chapter Six

Selling Value-Add

"More expensive, and worth it."

It may seem counterintuitive, but the lowest price is not always the deciding factor in a purchasing decision. We see lots of good examples of this fact in everyday life.

- Starbucks: People stand in line at Starbucks to pay $4 for a cup of coffee. They could go to Sally's Café and have their cups refilled all morning for $1.25, but they are willing to pay more for a premium brand.
- Lexus: Essentially, this car is a Toyota with "bling." They share the same manufacturing platform ("platform manufacturing" involves common design, engineering, and production efforts), but Lexus is the premium brand, and people are happy to pay for the luxury.
- Apple: Who is more passionate about their premium brand than Apple users? iPod, iPad, iPhone, iMac; fans of these products are willing to pay twice as much for a MacBook as they would pay for an equivalent PC laptop. Apple customers understand the value of a premium brand and would never consider moving back downstream to more generic (i.e., "clunkier") options.

At Starbucks, customers get more than a cup of coffee. They get premium blends with all sorts of flavor options, baked goods, comfortable ambience, and wireless networks. With Lexus, customers know to expect a better ride, a quieter interior, a better "fit and finish," and personalized service. With Apple, customers get imaginative technology, common-sense interfaces, and an unmatched element of Cool. These companies demonstrate and deliver value-add that fosters loyalty in their customers for their very profitable products.

Another interesting characteristic of people purchasing premium brands is that they rarely return to the lower-priced alternative. Starbucks customers don't go back to Sally's Café for a lukewarm cup of dishwater, and a Lexus owner probably won't trade his car in for a Camry. With great confidence, I predict that you will never see an Apple fan trading his or her machine for a Dell. When you establish your company as the premium brand, your customers are less likely to return to the lower-priced option.

You see, no matter what a customer tells you at first, price is rarely the top priority. Ask the customer in an offhanded way; he will confirm it. Here is a story to demonstrate a technique I've used successfully to confirm that price is not the top priority:

I was in Maryland competing for a large technology project at one of the premier printing companies in the state. After spending several hours describing our offering to management, I went to the whiteboard and wrote the following:

- *Price*
- *Performance*
- *Scalability*
- *Reliability*
- *Support*

Then I went back to the conference table and handed the marker to the decision maker. I explained that we had learned that the items listed on the board are the top five things our customers take into consideration when purchasing technology.

"We need you to help us by prioritizing these considerations in the order that works for you. With your guidance, we can create a solution customized to meet your specific needs."

I've used this technique too many times to count. In all those times, I have never seen a customer place price as the top priority.

One of the fundamentals of selling at a higher price (for higher profits) is to package products into "bundles" or "solutions." This implies that the customer has a specific need that you understand, and your expertise enables you to provide a custom offering that meets that need. A combination of products and services results in an offering that cannot be "shopped" or compared with a competitor's product. You see this in all types of businesses: insurance companies offering free needs assessments and discounted rates when combining coverage; or a barber shop that washes your hair and softens your beard with a hot towel before the complimentary shave. The barber will charge more for the actual haircut than the competition, but the service bundle adds value for which you are willing to pay.

This is standard operating procedure in the technology industry, where we call our bundles "solutions." When a solution's components are listed one by one, or itemized, it is easy for a customer to compare the price of your offering with competitive offerings. This removes any mystery surrounding your solution — thereby making it a commodity — and will inevitably reduce your profit margin. But when several products and services are combined to provide a "solution" to a common customer problem, we create mystery. One of my favorite sayings is:

There's margin in mystery.

Here's an example of a technology "solution"; the concept works for any business …

I had a customer in South Texas who ran a large printing company that needed to protect a very large amount of data. We had installed a tape library which, at the time, was the standard approach to data protection but was too slow for this customer's needs. He needed his data back online as quickly as possible, and tape was pretty slow. This was a business problem that needed a solution.

Our company did some engineering and came up with a technology bundle that solved the customer's problem. It was priced based on the solution's value and not its cost. If we had line itemed each component of the solution, we would have removed its mystery and our customer would have been able to "shop" us to the competition. By maintaining the mystery of our solution, however, we were able to protect our secrets and our margins. Our unique approach to solving this common problem allowed us to duplicate the profitable sale many times over with referrals provided by the satisfied customer. We were more expensive than the competition, but worth it.

While this example deals with bundling products to provide a technology solution, any business or industry can use the same philosophy to create mystery and increase margins. A restaurateur offers a solution to a dining problem by bundling wine and a dessert with the meal and creates extra margin in the process. Automobiles are sold with packaged "extras" that increase the selling price and the profits. Almost everyone will pay more to get more, and understanding that basic truth is the foundation of "value-add" sales. All you need to do is clearly demonstrate the value-add and you can avoid the price wars that kill small businesses.

Another way to add value to your offering is through superior service. Most buyers take it for granted that a low-priced product comes with low-quality service. Some low-priced products are actually purchased as "throwaways," with the purchaser knowing that it won't last long and comes with no guarantees. On the other hand, many quality businesses have been built around products backed with superior service. Some premium brands in the automobile industry feature free maintenance for the first three years. My technology company provided such high-quality service that our customers were willing to pay extra for the peace of mind that came with dealing with us.

Toward the end of our first year in business, we were able to convince a sophisticated account in Dallas, Texas, to allow our small company to compete for his business. We assured him that our service would balance out any concerns he had with our company's size.

Three weeks after installation, I received a call in the middle of the night. The caller was very upset. He reported that two of our computers had failed and they had work to produce for the next day's jobs. He asked if I could be there "first thing in the morning" to repair the machines.

"No, sir," I replied. "I don't think you can wait that long. Let me throw on my jeans and I'll be there in 30 to 40 minutes."

There was silence on the other end of the line. After a few seconds, he asked,

"You're coming now?"

"You need the work ready in the morning, right?"

"Yes."

"And you're running a third shift to get it done?"

"Yeah, that's right."

"The way I see it, your boss will be mighty upset if he pays for a third shift and doesn't get that work done in time. I'll be there in a little while. Could you put some coffee on?"

I got to the shop just before 3 a.m. I had the computers repaired in less than an hour, and the work was ready when the boss arrived. The shift supervisor raved about the technician who came in at 3 a.m. to fix the machines for the production run. The boss looked at me and smiled.

"This is no technician, Stuart," he said to the supervisor. "This

is the man who owns the company. He came at 3 in the morning and we're up and running? I guess we will be working with these guys for awhile."

I didn't want to get out of bed at 2 o'clock in the morning and drive across town to repair my machines, but I knew it was an opportunity to go "the extra mile," to put distance between us and our competition. The effort exceeded the customer's expectations and secured an account that spent hundreds of thousands of dollars with us over the next few years. They did it because they knew that we would go where the others would not ...

It is never crowded on "the extra mile."

This superior service mantra can be extended to any business. An automobile mechanic can provide car rentals to customers whose repairs will take more than a day. A florist can add a bit of baby's breath without charging an extra dollar. The restaurateur can remember a regular patron's name, and the grocery store bag boy can help you out to your car with your groceries. Many times, customers will decline the offers of assistance, but they will not forget them.

A friend of mine has been going to the same sandwich shop every day for the last four years and is likely to remain a customer for as long as the shop is in business. Every time she pulls up to the window, the lady says,

"Hey, Tawni. Will you be having the regular?"

It's not the sandwich that brings Tawni back; it's the feeling of personalized service.

In Summary: Selling Value-Add

- "Value-add" is what makes a company's products or services more expensive and worth it. Small businesses must sell and deliver value-add to avoid competing on price. Big Business will almost always have an advantage if price is the customer's buying criteria.
- People will pay more to get more; there are many examples of this fact in everyday life. People pay more for Starbucks coffee, Lexus automobiles, and Apple computer products than they might pay for competitive offerings. A customer who adopts a premium brand rarely returns to the lower-priced alternative.
- There's margin in mystery!
  - Bundle products to create solutions to consumer or business problems. A bundle should contain "secret ingredients" so that the solution cannot be itemized and "shopped." An example of a consumer solution is a "businessman's makeover" offered by a styling salon. It might include hair styling, hot towel treatment, shave, and a manicure. An example of a business solution is a computer backup system that includes a backup computer complete with backup software, setup, and maintenance.
  - Add services to products to create value. My favorite mechanic provides a rental car for me when he keeps my car for two or more days. He's more expensive than some of his competitors, but he does good work and makes it easy to have my car maintained.
- Do what the lower-priced competitor will not do for your customer. Provide the value you promise, the value for which the customer pays. Remember the saying that keeps me going when the competition starts to slow down: "It's never crowded on 'the extra mile.'"

Chapter Seven

Salescraft

"Selling with integrity, selling with style."

A craft is an art, trade, or occupation that requires special skill. "Salescraft" is the sum total of the special skills we require to be successful in our occupation as salespeople, and the best salespeople have turned sales into an art form.

Some are born with a talent for sales, but almost anyone can develop the skills necessary to sidestep selling on price. I refer to these skills as salescraft. I present them in this single chapter, although they fall into two distinct groups: basic salescraft and advanced salescraft. Basic salescraft addresses the fundamentals, such as how to dress and what [not] to drive, and how to build relationships that support your value-add. Advanced salescraft deals with learning to speak PeopleSpeak, asking yes/yes questions, and negotiating for discounts. Each deals with a specific protocol that works to create comfort and confidence in the prospect's mind.

These are guidelines; feel free to personalize them with your own sense of style. Basic salescraft may seem overly simple to you at first, but as you observe other (less professional) salespeople, you will see that these guidelines are often forgotten or mistakenly deemed unnecessary. Advanced salescraft is certain to bring a smile to your face and new levels of achievement in your chosen profession.

BASIC SALESCRAFT
How to Dress

The general rule is to dress one step nicer than your audience. If you're invited to the customer's company picnic and the employees are wearing shorts and T-shirts, you should wear nice jeans and a polo shirt. If the dress code for a meeting is business casual, you should arrive in slacks or a skirt with a sweater or a shirt. You may choose not to wear a tie if they're wearing jeans and short-sleeve shirts, but stick with slacks instead of jeans. Obviously these general rules of thumb are gender-neutral. The objective isn't to make yourself out to look better than your customers; just keep it one step up from your audience — out of respect. Let them know that they are important and that you always put your best foot forward for them. Your attire demonstrates a professionalism that they will come to respect and appreciate.

What [Not] to Drive

There's nothing worse than a salesperson who parks out front of an account in a $100,000 car. It screams to the customer,

"Look where all your money is going. You're paying too much for my services!"

If you're driving a car that cost more than his car, you're alienating the customer. I learned this early on in my career when an old man who looked like a farmer walked into my boss's office. Before he even said hello, he asked my boss who was driving the Cadillac sitting in the parking lot. My boss told him it belonged to one of the hired hands. The farmer sat down, broke out his briefcase, and exposed himself as one of the investors in the company. He wanted to make sure that his money wasn't going to waste. (My boss had a Cadillac and a little Porsche, too. But he drove his SUV to the meeting that day!)

How to Pick Up the Tab

It is standard practice to take prospects and customers out to lunch. There is something about breaking bread together that makes for better relationships. It goes without saying that the prospect never pays for lunch. Here's a technique that avoids "I'll get it" arguments and, at the same time, shows a little style.

When first walking into the restaurant, allow your guests to lead the way to the table. Palm your credit card (have it hidden in your hand) and hand it to the waitress or hostess as you trail your friends to the table. Communicate your intentions with words or a wink; they will understand. When the meal is finished, the waiter or waitress will bring the bill directly to you and will likely address you by name. Your guests will be surprised and somehow seem more appreciative. Undoubtedly, they will be certain to remember your style.

Remember, it's the little things in life that count: not just picking up the check, but doing it in a respectful, appreciative way. People don't often remember all the things you say, but they always remember how you made them feel. Cultivate and master the application of Class.

Render an Opinion

Have you ever been to a restaurant and asked the waiter for a recommendation, only to get the "Everything is good" response? I am immediately disappointed. I ask the waiter because he's an expert, and I want an expert's opinion. If he doesn't want to risk being too specific, he could say, "If you are in the mood for fish, the cedar plank salmon is always good; but the most popular beef is our rib eye." The honest, informative reply is the answer I want to hear.

When a customer comes into your place of business, offer him or her benefit of your expertise. Render an opinion. Your specialized knowledge is part of your premium brand; it is part of what makes you more expensive and worth it. Customers ask you questions because they value what you have to say; your expert opinion is a component of your company's value-add.

How to Build the Right Relationship

Your ability to sell value-add is a function of your ability to build a personal relationship with your prospect or customer. A salesperson who wins with a low price will inevitably lose to a lower price. It is only a matter of time; there is no loyalty when a buying decision is based solely on price. And do you know what the customer will tell the losing salesperson?

He'll say, "Don't take it personally; it's only business."

Never believe that statement, friends. If you're doing things right,

> *Business* is *personal.*
> *It always has been. It always will be.*

Think back to Main Street America in the 1950s. A town like the fictional Mayberry R.F.D., where everyone knew everyone and your reputation meant something. In those days, building a business relationship meant more than taking someone out to lunch. It meant spending time in a customer's place of business to learn how it worked, how the people worked, how they cared for their customers, and what their customers expected. It meant offering ideas as well as products that would make your customer's business life a little easier. In spite of all the changes we've seen during the last 60 years, the same methodology is valued today. To build a lasting business relationship you have to invest your time and attention into your customer's business and develop an intimate understanding of how the whole thing works. You become a "virtual" manager and an important part of the organization. And when you've built a meaningful relationship with that customer, it's not just business anymore; it's personal.

ADVANCED SALESCRAFT
PeopleSpeak

Building a long-term relationship is a two-way street. As discussed in Chapter Five, listening is probably the most important aspect of this process. But we give information, too. When we give information to a current customer or prospect, we need to deliver it in a language they will understand. We need to learn to speak their language, and we learn to speak their language by listening.

I worked with a man for many years who was a master of blending in with the customer's environment. After spending five minutes with prospects or customers, he would have them believing that he grew up in the same county as they did and listened to the same sermons. He was a chameleon, and his talent put both blue-collar workers and CEOs equally at ease with him. He called his secret "PeopleSpeak."

The objective is to learn to speak the way they speak; not mimicking the customer, but "fitting in" to his or her mode of conversation. Know what topics (interests), aspects of business (technical, financial, managerial), technical terms, and business attitudes they value. By listening, we are able to learn a great deal about the prospect's business, worry points, risk tolerance, and upcoming growth plans. We gather all kinds of good data that we can use to begin to build a business relationship. If you're listening for it, you get a feel for gathering this communication data when you're doing your preliminary questioning.

Use PeopleSpeak to build a quick, intimate relationship with a business prospect. Speaking the way a person speaks at work, asking questions, and genuinely listening are the best ways I know to win a person's trust. People buy from people they trust, and we trust people who speak our language. We're more comfortable when we're around "like folk." So a good salesperson listens, asks a few questions, blends in, and listens some more — all the while getting a handle on the PeopleSpeak of the prospect.

Yes/Yes Questions

We ask questions to get the information we need to work toward a sale. We ask questions to get prospects talking because they like to talk about their companies and they really like people who listen. We ask questions to learn about their interests, values, and specific vernacular. All of these questions are used as we work toward and guide the prospect to the sale. All of these questions are asked for a reason, but the most useful customer responses come when I ask yes/yes questions.

Yes/yes questions are like the question you hear at the grocery store checkout:

"Paper or plastic?"

No matter how you answer the question, you're going to get a bag. We want to ask questions that subconsciously imply a purchase by the prospect. We want that prospect to get used to saying "Yes."

Here's one of my favorite yes/yes questions. If you're prospecting for an appointment, you might ask ...

"Would you like to meet over lunch, or is meeting at your office better?"

Regardless of the option selected, you're going to get an appointment.

If you are selling a service contract, your question might be ...

"Do you want to pay for service monthly, or receive the discount by paying a year in advance?"

Do you see how it works? No matter how the prospect answers, he or she is signing up for service. Another yes/yes question could be ...

"Do you want French fries or onion rings with that hamburger, sir?"

If you use the yes/yes question technique properly, you're not asking the customer if he or she wants your product. You are asking the customer which product he wants.

Yes/yes questions get yes/yes answers.

It is important to ask the right questions, and it is important to ask them the right way. The right questions to ask are yes/yes questions that lead you to lots of sales.

How to Negotiate a Discount

I have had many customers ask for discounts on the purchase of products or services. In some cultures, it is considered weak and foolish not to haggle for a better price. People want to feel like they're getting a good deal. In my opinion, granting a wish for a discount is acceptable, but only if you negotiate for something in return.

We were working with a software company to sell a complete technology solution to a customer in Florida. We were selling the hardware, which included a sizable data storage system. After making his pitch, the software salesman handed his proposal over to the customer. The last page of the proposal was the Discount Page, wherein the salesman listed the discounts applied to every component of his proposal. The discount reduced the software price by almost 30 percent, lowering the purchase price from $120,000 to $87,500.

After the software presentation, we delivered our proposal. When we finished, the customer looked through our documentation and asked,

"Where is the discount page?"

To which I replied,

"We would be happy to negotiate a discount with you, sir. In exchange for what?"

This caught the customer off-guard. Being a small businessman himself, he knew that profit is a precious thing, hard-earned and hard to give up. Instinctively, he knew that ours was a reasonable response.

He replied, "What do I have that is of value to you?"

I said, "Several things, perhaps. I can discount my price in ex-change for a purchase order today. Or an agreement to pay 10 days net. Maybe we could work something out if you pay for the first year of the service contract in advance. I'm confident we can find something that works for both of us."

I'm not a big fan of "It works every time" statements, but this may be an exception. Offering a discount of value to the customer in exchange for something of value to you knocks him off-balance. It tells the customer two things; that you value her business, and that your product is fairly priced. It is bad business to give away profit, but you can trade for things you value if the customer wants a discount. The customer in the story respected our reasonable request and he agreed to pay us "net 10 days" in exchange for a fair discount. This was a far better deal than the one "negotiated" by our software partners and, in some subtle way, helped us to build a different relationship with the customer — one of mutual respect.

As you can see, salescraft includes the basic behaviors and niceties that work together with more sophisticated techniques to build your reputation as a professional. Salescraft demonstrates to the customer that you are serious about your work and sincere in your intentions. Once you make it through the first five minutes, you can begin to leverage your knowledge and sales skills to build a lasting, mutually beneficial relationship with that customer — a relationship that will provide you with both sales revenue and referrals. When you use salescraft to build relationships with a number of customers, you build a lasting and fulfilling career.

BASIC SALESCRAFT

- Dress one step nicer than your audience. The intention is not to show them up, but rather to demonstrate respect for them, their business, and the business event.
- Never drive the most expensive car in your customer's lot. The customer will feel like he's paying too much for your product or service. It's true that people buy from successful people, but be humble with your success.
- Pick up the tab before you sit down. Discreetly hand your credit card to the hostess or waitress as you follow your guests to the table. It is an unforgettable statement of style; you will be surprised how long it stays in your customer's mind.
- When asked, offer your professional opinion. It's part of your "value-add" — the expertise for which the customer will pay. There's nothing as disappointing as an expert without an opinion.
- Always remember: Business *is* personal. As a small business that values its relationship with its customers, business is (and will always be) personal. It is an important differentiator.

ADVANCED SALESCRAFT

- Speak the language that the prospect speaks at work. Ask questions and listen to learn; you don't want to mimic the prospect, but you do want to speak at a similar technical, social, and personal level as the individual with whom you are engaged.
- Prospects buy from people they trust, and they trust people who speak their language. How you speak is how you "deal"; get it right.
- Ask yes/yes questions to set up the sale. Yes/yes questions

are structured to elicit a positive response from the prospect. The best example of a yes/yes question is the one asked by the grocery store bagger: "Paper or plastic?" No matter your answer, you're leaving with a bag.

- Negotiate a discount; never give one away. You can trade a discount for an immediate sale, better payment terms, or an extended service contract. Whatever you do, don't give away profit.

Chapter Eight

Competing
with Big Business

"Sell your premium brand;
what makes you different and better?"

I t is simple [but not easy] to compete with and outsell Big Business. Convince the prospects and customers in your community that they prefer small business quality to Big Business quantity. Create empathy; help them see that your small business is not unlike their small business and therefore you're better able to understand their problems than a multibillion-dollar, multinational mega-corporation. Once they make that connection, you've established a relationship that your small business can leverage.

The strength of Big Business is in its size and resources. The power of its marketing engines and its ability to purchase in colossal volumes (which enables Big Business to deliver unbeatably low prices) is an advantage in its efforts to gain market share. Big Business doesn't sell products; it markets them. Frequent exposure of Big Business brands captures the attention of consumers and saturates them with low-price messaging.

Small businesses do not have the marketing budgets to counter mega-brand advertising. As individual companies, we are hopelessly outgunned when it comes to advertising. However, there is a chance to compete for the customer's attention if we collaborate. For example, recent efforts by small businesses to organize Buy Local campaigns have proven effective in the campaign to regain mindshare and reestablish the value of small businesses to their local communities. They have also proven to be a very effective way for small, local retailers to improve sales. We can't sell the individual value of each small business participating in the program when we market collectively; there won't be advertising space or time for the custom bike shop, the florist, and all the other small businesses to air their individual ads. But collaborative efforts like Buy Local campaigns communicate the value of small business to consumers and can be effective counterstrikes to Big Business's marketing punch. When local merchants and customers see you as a small business, you gain a measurable advantage.

Getting involved in Buy Local campaigns is as simple as contacting your local or regional organization. If nothing else, post "Buy Local" signs in your place of business. It is a powerful campaign that has everyone's attention.

In many ways, our size is our advantage. The large corporations lack agility; they cannot respond to market changes with the speed of a small business. Mega-retailers create powerful brand recognition but lack the emotional connection of entrepreneurial businesses. Except for their brands, they lack any emotional bond with a customer at all. We need to remind potential customers that *our* small business is like *their* small business.

This emotional advantage is the single most powerful weapon we can leverage in our effort to differentiate ourselves from Big Business. When competing for a sale to a smaller company, we can use it to create empathy. We remind the prospect that we are peers. Our small company better understands his needs, whether those needs are for specialized products or responsive support. We can support each other and provide referrals for each other. We can, in fact, create a real relationship (as opposed to the superficial "here today, gone tomorrow" affair delivered by large, impersonal corporations). I use the following illustration to drive home this point:

I was working on a sale with a small company in Minneapolis, Minnesota. They were planning to upgrade their computer systems. Representatives from the Big Computer Company (BCC) had already visited the facility and made a compelling pitch. Their equipment was of a very good quality and their pricing very competitive. We had the expertise to compete with their offering, but BCC had lower pricing.

After outlining the technical side of our proposal, I went up to the whiteboard in the conference room and drew a large rectangle with a blue marker. I then laid the blue marker back into the tray and picked up a red marker. I turned to the decision makers seated at the conference table and said,

"This rectangle represents the local revenues of our competition. Not national or international revenues, just the money that comes from our region."

I turned to the whiteboard and drew a red line parallel to and just above the bottom blue line; the two lines were actually touching one another.

"This line represents your contribution to BCC's revenues. Remember, please, that this is a conceptual drawing. Your percentage contribution to our competitor's revenue is actually less than this; I just don't have a marker thin enough to make the drawing to scale. No disrespect intended, but your sale is not an important part of our competitor's bottom line."

I laid the red marker back into the tray and picked up the black marker. I drew a line approximately one-third of the way up from the bottom of the rectangle.

"This line represents the value of your contribution to our company. It's not actually a third of our revenue, but it is of much greater value to us than it is to our competition. And we will respond to your questions, concerns, and need for support as though you were our largest customer. We are a small business — like your small business — and we cannot afford to lose a single customer. You are more than an account to us; you are an important part of our future. When you make the decision to purchase from us, you will be treated like our largest and most important customer."

This approach leverages a common bond between our small business and that of our prospective customer. It is a bond that cannot be established by a mega-retailer, no matter the discounts and promises it offers. There is no affinity between your local hardware store and Home Depot or Walmart. There is no comparing the advice you receive from a local photo supply shop with that provided by the teenage part-timer watching the clock at a big box store. When the added value that comes from frequenting local businesses is demonstrated and acknowledged, the customer will understand that small business is worth a little more.

There is no community of interests shared by Big Business and small customers.

Intuitively, we all know the importance of supporting America's small businesses. The customer's investment in small business is not just to obtain better products and services, but to sustain growth and maintain business diversity. This information should become part of your sales pitch when competing with Big Business.

Small Business has to sell the things it makes and the things for which it stands.

Attract customers, earn their attention, know what you have to offer, and articulate that offering. In order to compete with Big Business, you must call the customer's attention to the things that make you different.

Differentiate: Sell attitude with enthusiasm.

Here's a personal experience to illustrate the point:

My business partner and I were competing with two MNCs (multinational companies — like Dell or IBM or Hewlett-Packard) for a large contract with an international printing company. We made it to the final cut but had an uncomfortable feeling that we were the "token small business" in the deal. Communications dwindled as we approached the award date. We felt that we needed to get the decision maker's attention, so we went to the local boot store (not too far of a drive in Texas) and purchased a pair of plain black cowboy boots. We put only one of the boots in a box (so the prospect would not think them a gift) and wrote a note to place on top of the boot:

"We have the right technology. We have the right experience. We are the right team for this job. Please, just let us get our foot in the door. We promise we won't let you down."

We FedEx'd the boot to arrive at the prospect's location the following day. Immediately after the lunch hour, the prospect phoned us. He was in a very good mood.

"I don't know what to say 'bout this boot, boys," he chuckled. "You wanna get your foot in the door? You get on the first plane to Atlanta tomorrow and I'll give ya one more shot at this job."

We got that last shot, we hit the target, and we won the deal. The boot didn't win the job, mind you; we had to deliver the product and support that we had committed to in the tender. But, by shipping that boot with an attention-getting note, we were able to differentiate ourselves from the MNCs. We were able to demonstrate that his business meant more to us than it did to the competition and that our approach to service would be different. That act in and of itself opened the door to earning a $250,000 job for one of the world's largest printing companies. Seven years later, that account is still a profitable source of good revenue.

Service is the not-so-secret weapon of small business. No matter how it tries to duplicate the personalized interest we show in each and every customer, Big Business will forever remain a cold and impersonal option.

Service is sometimes as important as the product itself. This is especially true when selling technical products such as computers, mountain bikes, automobiles, or home electronics. I'll give you an example:

Anyone selling technology has had to compete with the "Four-Hour Response Contract" offered by the large technology resellers. The Four-Hour Response Contract means that the customer's service needs will be addressed in four hours or less, guaranteed. On the surface, this is very attractive to a customer. Dell offers its local technicians, Best Buy has the Geek Squad, and other resellers have their teams. It creates a challenge for small companies in the technology business. How can we compete with the support resources of companies like Dell and Best Buy?

I was sitting in my office trying to find a way to combat this strategy when I overheard a conversation that one of our technicians was having with a customer.

"You can afford to wait four hours? You call me with a problem and I'll be on it like a chicken on a June bug!"

Trae is the lead technician in our organization. He is a quiet man, but will not hesitate to share strong opinions on technology and his craft.

"Come on, man," he said as he needled one of his favorite accounts. "Are you telling me you would be willing to wait half a day for someone to check out your broken business computer? That you are willing to pay for the privilege of waiting four hours for a guy who doesn't give a damn about you and your problem?

If I can't fix it in a half-hour, I'll replace the machine before you go home. There's no cost and you don't have to sign a contract. We call it Great Service and it's free to all our customers. Four-Hour Response Contract. Seriously, would you really pay to wait when you can get my immediate attention for free?"

The point here is the same as that made throughout this book: You've got to tell the customer about the things that make you different. It's important — it's critical — to differentiate your offering, but it's just as important to communicate. Explain the things that make you different in a way that the customer will understand.

Sometimes, a customer or prospect has already made a purchase from the bigger competitor. He may actually be happy buying from a superstore. But that doesn't mean that the customer is lost. Chances are, the big company's lack of personal attention will upset the customer at some point in time. In this situation, the appropriate tactic is to position your company as the "backup plan."

When competing with a large, low-cost company, I have found it effective to respond to the customer's "No, I'm happy with my current supplier," with:

"I understand. I can respect the relationship you have with our competitors. I would want the same loyalty from you myself. But every good businessperson needs a second option, a reliable backup plan. And I would like to be your backup plan, just in case you ever find yourself in need. Can I leave my card with you just in case you ever find yourself needing an option?"

Many things can be accomplished with this "soft sell" response. First and foremost, it takes the pressure off the customer.

It demonstrates professionalism by respecting his existing relationship and it reminds him of the wisdom in keeping an option close at hand in case his existing vendor stumbles. Then we can wait and prepare until the opportunity presents itself.

In this chapter, we have discussed strategies and tactics for competing with and differentiating ourselves from Big Business. We cannot compete on price; we may win a job or two, but we won't last very long. We win by turning the tables on Big Business; we sell our small business products and services as premium brands. We convince the customer that our higher prices reflect higher-quality products and services, and that Big Business's low prices come from lower-quality products and support. Moreover, we have a "real world" understanding of the customers' business problems because we're small businesses, too. The mega-corporations cannot understand or empathize with the needs of a small business. Once the customer makes the connection, a relationship is established that your small business can leverage for many years to come.

In Summary: Competing with Big Business

- Big Business will always get the sale if the buying decision is based on price.
- Big Business will capture prospective customers' attention with its mass marketing.
- Overcome the marketing power of Big Business by getting involved in collaborative marketing efforts with other small businesses, like Buy Local campaigns.
- Position your products and services as premium brands; people will pay more to get more, and rarely return to the lower-priced option.
- Explain those things that make your products and services different and demonstrate that which differentiates you. Do not assume that the customer sees the value in the differentiation. Communicate in PeopleSpeak.
- Pull the customer closer by establishing an emotional bond; illustrate the similarities of your companies and show how that helps you better understand the customer's problems and needs.
- Leverage the emotional bond by reminding the customer that Big Business has no empathy for her business, nor is it interested in understanding her needs. The only relationship Big Business wants with your customer is a transactional relationship.
- Demonstrate your enthusiasm for winning her business, and communicate your eagerness to provide superior support in order to keep her business.

Chapter Nine

Cultivating a Sales Culture

"You've got culture, whether you know it or not."

I learned something powerful from a saleswoman in Dallas. She prefaced the lesson by describing her prospecting effort to land an important account in town. She had asked friends and customers for referrals in that organization and, having finally solicited a strong referral, enjoyed a productive conversation with a person in the purchasing department. My friend asked questions and listened until she found a problem she could solve for the prospect. They agreed to meet the following week, exchanged contact information, and booked an appointment for lunch at a restaurant close to the prospect's place of business. Unfortunately, she didn't win the sale. In fact, she never met the prospect in person because they never went to lunch. They never went to lunch because the sales prospect was mistreated by another member of the saleswoman's company. It happened that the prospect called the next afternoon and asked to speak to the saleswoman. The prospect was put on hold and forgotten. An inattentive receptionist failed to provide a quality service, and that is how the prospect perceived the saleswoman's company.

"If this is how I'm treated BEFORE the sale, how bad will it be AFTER they get my money?"

Disasters like the one I just described can be prevented when every employee understands and executes their part in the sales process. Getting the entire team pulling in the same direction is the direct result of having a sales culture. Prospects are seldom neglected when there is a sales culture guiding a company.

In this chapter, I describe how an organization's untapped sales resources come together and fuse into something powerful and sustainable. I show how employees can grow beyond their isolated, individual responsibilities and contribute to the company's all-important sales effort. Then, as it is often said, the whole becomes greater than the sum of its parts. This cohesiveness is not the result of a particular management style or policy, or the delivery of a well-crafted corporate directive. It is evidence of the existence of a sales culture. *Merriam-Webster* defines culture as "the set of shared attitudes, values, goals, and practices that characterizes an institution or organization." When the shared attitudes, values, goals, and practices are sales-related, there is a company sales culture. "Culture" is more than an important word; it is a very powerful tool.

Culture dictates behavior; this is evident in societies throughout the world and throughout the history of mankind. America's culture of freedom and independence fosters confident, free-speaking individuals who step outside the boundaries of common thought and action to innovate. Other cultures are more restrictive; there are societies whose cultures dictate submissive and obedient behavior, and some that promote a more stoic and strict environment. There are cultures that place emphasis on religion and ritual, and cultures that evangelize social responsibility. In each case, the society's culture dictates its behavior.

The same is true for organizational culture. A company's culture consists of all the written and unwritten rules about how things happen in the organization. There are obvious parallels between organizational culture and social culture. Both express or imply rules for behavior, acceptable conduct, and values and beliefs. An organization's culture serves to establish its standard for behavior and supports its institutional values. Culture is an important aspect of an organization, and one that is too often overlooked and undervalued.

Culture, as it applies to the contents of this book, is a powerful tool that should be harnessed to increase small business sales. Clearly, the ideas in this book are sales fundamentals directed primarily at field salespeople. However, they benefit managers in that they provide a foundation on which to build a sales culture. In a nutshell: If your organization needs to increase its sales, it needs to increase its organizational sales effort — not just the efforts of a single salesperson or the sales department. One of the great failings of sales managers is their tendency to look at salespeople and say, "You need to sell more." It is far more realistic — and productive — to look at the organization as a whole and say, "We need to sell more."

It is important to understand and accept the fact that selling is a team sport. Everyone in an organization is in some form or fashion responsible for sales, and it is the sales manager's (and, ultimately, the general manager's) responsibility to make sure that everyone on the team participates in the sales effort. Successful sales organizations are those that cultivate and embrace a sales culture.

"Culture? We don't need no stinking culture!"

I can't tell you how many people I've heard say this in response to my suggestion that they cultivate a company sales culture. It is as if they think culture is superfluous, like sponsoring office massages or Friday Tai Chi in the parking lot. Many are convinced that organizations function fine without it.

You've got culture, whether you know it or not.

Even today, the behavior of your employees is a function of the written and unwritten rules that are embraced and exhibited by management and ownership. And management's written and unwritten rules for getting things done in your place of business are telltale signs of a corporation's culture. Whether you are aware of it or not, your company has a culture all its own.

For example, the penny-pinching boss who spends most of his business time searching for savings creates a frugal mindset and mood among his employees. Following the boss's lead, everyone is looking for a cheaper way to get things done. Obviously, the Purchasing Department is always negotiating for a better price, sometimes trading quality for cost. Shipping and Receiving inevitably selects the slowest method of shipment, even when returning product to service customers. Human Resources may select inferior benefits to lower costs, in spite of the impact that decision may have on company morale or motivation. And while this is good from a balance sheet point of view, quality of work, product, and customer service can suffer. If the boss is aware of this, he or she may make time to better define the rules of conduct. He or she may refine the rules to say, "Save money at all costs, except at the cost of the customer." Or not. In either case, they have established a culture within the organization that dictates the behavior of its people.

Another boss may state that sales is the responsibility of every employee, and she provides specific training and tools for every employee so that they can meet their own clear objectives on a timeline. She works with her employees to help them understand their roles in the company's sales effort and to generate enthusiasm. She encourages those who share her enthusiasm and reassures those who are uncomfortable with the challenge. She invests in training to support the team and brings in outside help to coach the participants. She is establishing a sales culture — sharing all those written and unwritten rules about how things get done — that will inevitably lead to more customers, more sales, and more profit.

> *Leadership establishes the*
> *foundation for culture.*

One thing you have probably noticed is that it is very difficult (if not impossible) to change a company's culture without someone in management championing that change. The obvious candidate for implementing and managing a cultural transition is the company owners, general managers, and sales managers who want to create a sales culture in their organizations. To create a sales culture, the champion must have a vision that is clearly articulated and includes simple, realistic expectations. It must be presented formally to the entire team — as a corporate proclamation — and enthusiastically and repeatedly shared with employees in their offices, in the hall, and in the break room.

Another requirement for building a sales culture is to identify those who can and will participate, and to show them how to do what they need to do to meet the company's realistic expectations. That is not to say that the organization's expectations are not challenging, only that they are achievable. The transformation to a sales culture will not happen overnight, so the steady achievement of realistic goals is needed to build the confidence of those without sales experience.

Let's discuss a few specifics:

The Receptionist. This individual is generally not one of the more highly paid people in the company. The receptionist is not tightly supervised. He or she usually sits at a long desk in the lobby or near the door with a desktop computer and a phone. He or she receives calls and forwards them to the appropriate party. Generally, receptionists are also generalists. They order lunch for guests, perform odd jobs for management, and look for lots of information.

Please notice that I defined the job as "receives calls and forwards them"; there was no mention made of HOW to receive them. Some receptionists are naturally cheerful and greet every caller as if that person were their friend. Some receptionists are bored with their job (and not particularly thrilled with their life, it would seem) and they answer every call as though it were the

IRS. Even the perky receptionist has bad days, but a sales culture would dictate that — bad day or good — every incoming call is received as pleasantly and professionally as possible. The receptionist should be trained to understand that the position is critical to the sales process. Every caller is a potential customer, and the receptionist is the first salesperson with whom the caller communicates. Receptionists in a company that has a sales culture know that they are salespeople, too.

Technicians/Technical Support Personnel. These folks usually deal with customers who are having problems with the product. Customers can be clueless (as to how the product is supposed to work), frustrated (because they can't get the product working), or mad (because they feel the technician somehow slighted him with the service). Technical support is a very stressful job that makes techs (generally speaking) less-than-perky people. Technicians/technical support personnel are more difficult to engage in the sales effort because they feel that many problems are caused by salespeople — selling the wrong product, selling things the products won't do, and selling products that do not yet exist. Nevertheless, technicians/technical support people interact with customers daily, and consequently they are part of the sales team.

People in technical support don't feel they have time to engage in idle chatter with the customer on the phone. They're right, of course. If, however, their conversation with a customer uncovered a need that would save the customer time, money, or additional headaches, that technician is in the ideal position to recommend something to meet that need. If a technician is repairing an outdated product for the third or fourth time, he or she should recommend that the customer get the product upgraded, and offer to "get the ball rolling" when they finish their call. A technician working in a sales culture would know that doing these sales-related things would generate some form of compensation, because the technician is a salesperson, too.

Employees without sales experience will need sales training.

Sometimes the sales management team can provide training. Most likely, the training will be contracted to a company or consultant who specializes in sales training. Moreover, the management team will need training on preparing for and initiating a migration to a corporate sales culture. It is critical that the company's decision makers support and participate in training. Training should be departmentally discrete; technicians or product support people will need a different kind of sales training than front office personnel, and sales management will need a program all its own. It doesn't end with training; those lessons need to be practiced and reinforced to become habit.

There is value in hiring outside expertise to assist management with its migration to a sales culture. Your group will need a coach to serve as an arbitrator, motivator, and sales culture sage. Trying to reinvent yourself by yourself can be difficult (if not impossible) to do. The right coach can validate your vision, bring credibility to it by sharing successful examples from other companies he has seen or with which he has worked, and help you steer clear of the bumps and potholes on the road to your success. It is easier for a coach to navigate the borderlands between departments. He has no history with the employees; there are no failures or favorites. The coach will give every participant his best effort and insight. He will build the participants' confidence with an early emphasis on low-risk sales activities, such as calling inactive customers, cross-selling, and up-selling. His objective is to see the owner's vision manifest itself in a new sales culture and an increase in sales.

*"Call it what you will,
incentives are what get people to work harder."*

This quote from Nikita Khrushchev defines motivation very well. Although the incentives to which he referred are unlikely to be used as inducements in an American corporation, people work hard for a reason. Most people work for money. There are some who labor for a cause and those who work for a better future (college students working on an education). But the vast majority of people in the workplace get up every day to earn a living. No amount of enthusiasm or promises of a better world are going to motivate them to do something they don't want to do (sell) for nothing. They work for money. Consequently, the organization's movement to a sales culture will need to be fueled with financial incentives and fair compensation to realize sustained success.

How does one design a compensation plan that addresses the individual needs and contributions of participating departments? What manner of compensation is acceptable? Will technicians and product support people be motivated by commission? Are secretaries and front office people money-motivated, too? Perhaps time off is of greater value to some of your team. It might be best to run sales campaigns for a specific period of time and reward the top performer(s) with a night on the town, a weekend retreat, or a trip to Cancun. If you want your team to enthusiastically embrace the concept of team sales and, subsequently, create an organizational sales culture, you need to solicit their ideas and input. You need to learn about the things they most value. Listen to their suggestions regarding fair compensation and remember that universal truth: "You've got to give to get." Ask the departments and individuals what motivates them to participate, and emotionally accept the fact that appropriate incentives are necessary for success.

In business, there is no such thing as "something for nothing." The privilege to sell and increase one's income comes with responsibilities. Sales accountability is perhaps the most difficult hurdle that your new team members will have to overcome. The privilege to sell and earn that which motivates comes with an obligation to sell, and everyone participating should be held accountable for their work. They have to give (acceptable prospecting and sales metrics) to get (commission and incentives), and this will make some members of your sales team uncomfortable. It will take time and reassurance, but they will come to understand.

So, you have shared your vision for a company with a sales culture. You have shared your enthusiasm with employees and identified those who are interested in participating. You've organized training and hired a coach. You've created unconventional compensation plans unique to each department and spelled out its important contribution to the bottom line. The only thing left to do is:

Burn the boats!

Legend has it that when the Spanish explorer Hernán Cortés landed in Veracruz in 1519, he ordered his men to burn the ships that were to carry the army home. The sight of the flaming ships removed any notion of retreat from the soldiers' hearts and any thoughts of surrender from their heads. The only way home was Victory. There could be no more dramatic a demonstration of commitment to a cause than this explorer's striking example.

Your commitment to building a sales culture in your company will be tested. There will be those who feel it wise to retreat. Some will want to surrender to the ease of their previous position and forget this whole "sales culture" thing. The first time a non-salesperson feels the sting of rejection, his or her commitment is going to waver. You will need to demonstrate *your commitment* to the change. You will need to reassure and redirect them. Get them additional training or one-on-one coaching. Invest in your people to demonstrate your commitment to a sales culture. Through your own example, demonstrate all the written and unwritten rules about how things get done in your sales-oriented company. Burn the boats — there is no alternative but victory.

In Summary: Cultivating a Sales Culture

■ Culture is defined as "the set of shared attitudes, values, goals, and practices that characterizes an institution or organization." Culture establishes the values of an organization and dictates behavior.

■ You've got culture, whether you know it or not. An organization's leadership establishes its culture.

■ The desired culture (especially in a small business that relies on value-add sales) is a sales culture. The leader in a sales culture shares all the written and unwritten rules about how things happen in a value-add sales environment.

■ Successful sales cultures are driven by incentives. Leadership must determine the best incentive for each department actively engaged in sales culture activity. As the company benefits from additional sales, so too should the employees responsible for generating those sales.

■ Leadership must demonstrate its commitment to the sales culture. A halfhearted commitment will yield halfhearted results. Declare your intention. Begin the training. Design the right compensation plans. Determine the objective and "burn the boats"!

Chapter Ten

Cultural Value of Legend and Lore

"A company's legend and lore form the foundation of its culture."

L et's start this chapter with two definitions.

Legend: a non-historical or unverifiable story handed down by tradition from earlier times and popularly accepted as historical.

Lore: the body of knowledge (especially of a traditional, anecdotal, or popular nature) on a particular subject.

I have had conversations with several of my friends and business associates about the value of legend and lore to a sales organization. Initially, very few understand what I'm trying to communicate with this concept. As the conversation continues, however, they invariably nod their heads in agreement.

A company's legend and lore form the foundation of its culture. They serve to form a company's identity and its sense of purpose. Legend provides vivid examples of the desired organizational behavior. Lore is the cumulative body of work that defines a company's favored conduct and style. Legend and lore guide managers and employees and motivate them to continue to achieve in the manner of their predecessors.

Once each week, David Burkhardt and I would spend the afternoon cold calling on prospects. It was very competitive; we took turns approaching prospects with our pre-approach (or what is often referred to as an "elevator pitch") and scored points for making appointments during the call. The man with the most appointments from cold calls at the end of the month won a free lunch. It was a great way to thicken a salesperson's skin, an action designed to make us more comfortable with rejection.

In a typical demonstration of Burkhardt's prospecting bravado, he pulled into a parking lot of a funeral home for the last call of the day.

"Oh, come on, David ... you're not thinking of going in there, are you?"

"Nobody knows the value of life insurance better than folks who work in a funeral home," Burkhardt said and smiled. "That's what I always say."

We walked inside the funeral home and Burkhardt was grinning like a Cheshire cat. I wasn't grinning at all; I wasn't worried about ghosts and zombies, but I was feeling a little spooked and completely out of place. Burkhardt asked the man who greeted us for "the boss." Shortly thereafter, a middle-aged man emerged from behind a curtain with long black shoulder-length hair and Elvis Presley sideburns. I was surprised by his appearance and his stereotypically somber demeanor. I was completely creeped out the minute I saw him and was anxious to leave as soon as possible. Burkhardt couldn't care less; he came in to sell life insurance and immediately launched into his pre-approach:

"Thanks for your time, sir. I'll start by saying that I don't have any reason to believe that you're in the market for life insurance. But I know that, when they buy, people prefer to buy insurance from people they trust or from a large reputable company. I came by to ask for an appointment so that, over time, I'll be the guy who has earned your trust when you're ready to buy life insurance."

The creepy funeral home director gave Burkhardt an appointment and, within two months, David sold him some life insurance.

This is one of those stories that helped Burkhardt become a legend at that life insurance company. I was there, so I know that it happened, but it was hard to believe for others. My peers would ask me to validate Burkhardt's story. Then, of course, they could see a copy of the insurance application that Burkhardt pinned up on the bulletin board after officially receiving the order. It was a shining example of the company president's desired organizational behavior.

It was also a "peer pressure engine."

"If Burkhardt can do it, every salesperson in this office can do it," said the company president. "Challenge yourselves. Get fit. Get busy."

The president was pressuring Burkhardt's peers to follow his lead. Legends set the bar for the next wave of high jumpers, and Burkhardt set the bar for cold calling. What call can one make any colder than a cold call at a funeral home? Burkhardt had become a legend, and the story became a part of our company lore.

Another benefit to cultivating legend and lore within the business is that it serves as a compass with which others can find their bearings. It provides an organization with clear direction so that it operates like a flock of geese. The geese all know where they are going and move in that direction together; alternating as a leader, a follower, or a scout and changing roles whenever necessary. The goose in the lead could change positions with another goose in the gaggle. When observing the unified "V" that the gaggle maintains, it is hard to determine which goose is in the lead at a particular point in time. A company's legend and lore establish the organization's direction and allow every "goose in the gaggle" an opportunity to lead.

A company's legend and lore identify culturally acceptable goals. They are guidelines for managers and salespeople to use in their efforts to realize their objectives. They provide examples of the means with which these goals can be achieved. Anecdotal evidence is the most convincing proof of concept. The most effective illustrations of management or sales concepts are found in the living examples of company legend and lore.

One of the most valuable aspects of legend and lore is that

they can be passed on to partners and customers. These anecdotes and examples of your past performance can attract new customers and establish a reputation for your company in a way that no marketing campaign can match. Let me share an example with you:

We had pursued a relationship with one of the largest potential customers for our products in the country. Unfortunately, the vice president in charge of managing vendor relationships already had a computer systems supplier, one of the more well-known companies of its type in the United States.

"We can respect and appreciate your loyalty, Larry. However, most organizations like to have a backup plan and we would like to be your emergency option."

He smiled a professional smile and accepted our business cards; we shook his hand and returned to Texas.

Several months later, there was a failure of one of these machines in a very high-profile account. His partner showed little enthusiasm for solving the problem and, in desperation, Larry called our small business for support. We called the customer but we were unable to repair the broken computer. We called Larry to update him on the situation.

"Isn't there anything you can do?" he asked.

"Sure, Larry," we replied. "We're preparing a replacement machine. We ship it out tonight for delivery tomorrow morning."

The machine in question was not an ordinary desktop computer. It was a high-performance server with an enormous amount of storage capacity. Replacing it in 12 to 14 hours would be difficult.

"That customer isn't going to buy a new machine, Taylor. He just wants to repair the one he owns."

"But he needs a machine tomorrow. We're not trying to sell him a computer, Larry; we're just trying to help him out."

"You're going to loan him a machine like the one he has? You

can build, test, and ship a computer like that overnight? How much is that going to cost?"

"It doesn't cost you anything, Larry. It's a loan. You pay the freight and make sure we get it back when he finishes his job."

We could tell by the lengthy silence on the phone that Larry was stunned. The offer seemed too good to be true.

Everything went according to plan. The customer completed the critical job and then returned our server as planned. Larry and his company looked like champions. Eventually, the primary supplier repaired its equipment, but our performance established our company as the premium brand. Over time, the story became legend within Larry's organization and was shared with their customers and prospects over and over for many years.

"You're not going to find another company like this one, Mr. Prospect," Larry's salespeople would say. "Their support is awesome. One time, a customer of ours was in an awful bind. Proactive Technologies built a replacement machine overnight and shipped it for next-day delivery. Our customer was up and running before lunchtime, finished the job, and shipped the system back to Texas. All we had to pay was freight. And it wasn't even their customer! They always do the right thing whether there's money in it or not. Why wouldn't you do business with a company like that?"

Our response to the customer's problem became legend in our industry. We established a reputation that we couldn't buy for any amount of money. No marketing campaign could compete with the positive exposure and demand creation that a simple instance of "giving to get" brought to our company. Therein lies the value of legend and lore to customers, and to partners and vendors as well.

A company's legend and lore form the foundation of its culture and forge its reputation in their industry. They shape and color a company's identity. Legend and lore define a company's conduct and style, and entice prospects to become your customers. Legend and lore guide managers and employees, and inspire them to follow in the footsteps of their predecessors. They identify the organizational path to success and provide examples for management and employees to follow.

In Summary: Cultural Value
of Legend and Lore

- Legend and lore form the foundation of a company's culture. They guide managers and employees, and motivate them to continue to achieve in the manner of their predecessors.

- Legend and lore can serve as a "peer pressure engine." Legends set the bar for the next wave of salespeople, support personnel, or other team members.

- A company's legend and lore establish the organization's direction.

- One of the most valuable aspects of legend and lore is that they can be passed on to partners and customers. These anecdotes and examples of your past performance can attract new customers and establish a reputation for your company in a way that no marketing campaign can match.

Chapter Eleven

Overcoming Internal Resistance

"Overcoming resistance within the organization
is no different than making any other sale."

Suppose you are a sales manager or a general manager of a company and you feel strongly that there is a need to increase sales. You believe that some of the ideas in this book (or others) could help your team and you have decided to implement some of those exciting new ideas. Perhaps you would like to put a new emphasis on prospecting, or hire a coach to work with employees, or develop a sales culture within your organization. You approach your boss for approval and, after outlining your plan for improvement, he or she says,

"No."

You are surprised. Taken aback. Why wouldn't the owner of a company (or its general manager) want to increase sales? Why wouldn't he or she want to make more money? Or increase the company's profits?

Well, all owners would like to increase sales and profits. What they don't want to do is fix something that (in their minds) isn't broken. If a company is profitable, its policies and procedures have been effective, and changing them could bring about undesired results. In many cases, owners or managers are unwilling to trade what works for what might not work. Change can be risky and, generally speaking, owners and managers are risk-averse.

When you want to implement change, it is imperative that you remember that most business owners and general managers — even departmental managers — look at things from a balance sheet point of view. They talk in terms of Risk Management and measurable Return on Investment. Arguing will not change their minds. It's better to negotiate for change.

To begin with, talk their talk. As discussed in Chapter Seven, you need to speak to them in a language that they can hear. Use terminology that gets their attention. Practice PeopleSpeak for management! Ask questions and listen as they lay out their point of view. Develop an understanding of their business fears and concerns. Step back from your excitement and be willing to negotiate; suggest implementing your project one manageable step at a time.

Suggest a Proof of Concept.

As opposed to a full-blown implementation, ask your boss to consider a proof of concept. Minimize his exposure to risk. Let the boss know that you feel strongly about the positive impact of your proposed alternative to her policies or procedures, and that you understand her concerns about changing things that have historically been productive and profitable. Lay things out on paper; try to minimize your emotion or enthusiasm and help the boss see the possibilities using her own language and perspective.

The key to overcoming internal resistance to your ideas to improve sales is to help the boss convince herself. It's a sale; practice the art of listening. Solicit her opinion. Convince her with the tools that she would use herself. If she is a "numbers" person, prepare a spreadsheet that illustrates the projected costs of your initiative and the potential return on that investment. If she is more of a "big picture" person, share with her trends in the industry and the anticipated growth in market share that could be realized by the company. Make note of her objections. Agree to project milestones and measurements of success, and agree (if you must) to "pulling the plug" on the project if she feels it's not working out.

Have your peers buy in as well. Invite them to a meeting and share your thoughts with them. Try not to present it as "a plan" or "a project"; that might create the impression that it is being forced upon them. Present the concept as some ideas you've come up with to help everyone make more money — a way to share the wealth. Then solicit their feedback (seeking both positive and negative opinions). Report back to them when you have consolidated their ideas and reviewed their collective opinion. Without their support, you will struggle to succeed with your plan.

Keep the boss and peer groups up to date. Report on the movement toward the agreed-upon milestones and revise the objectives as the boss sees fit. Be patient; slow, measurable progress will prove encouraging to all interested parties.

Deliver — on target and on time.

Reward the team for investing their money, time, and energy in the plan. Reward them with RESULTS! Resistance weakens when sales are made for a higher profit, and enthusiasm grows when bonuses are distributed to participating employees.

Overcoming resistance within the organization is no different than making any other sale. You must listen to the customer (i.e., the boss) and ask yes/yes questions. Clearly demonstrate the value you bring and be willing to go one step at a time. Then deliver — on target and on time. It will be easier to get approval for the next project when you have managed the first one to the boss's satisfaction.

In Summary: Overcoming Internal Resistance

- Bosses may resist your suggestions to change the way their products or services are sold.

- When trying to persuade them to consider your ideas, be sure to speak their language. Use terminology that communicates you understand their point of view.

- Offer to compromise with a proof-of-concept project. Illustrate your proposal using the tools the boss or manager uses — balance sheets for the "numbers guy" or industry trends for the "big picture" gal.

- Agree to project milestones and measurements of success, and agree (if you must) to "pulling the plug" on the project if it falls short of his or her expectations.

- Get your peers involved. Solicit their ideas and feedback. You will struggle to succeed without their support.

- Provide progress reports on a consistent basis. Solicit feedback and modify plans accordingly.

- Deliver — on target and on time. It will be easier to get approval for the next project when you have managed the first one to the boss's satisfaction.

Exemplars of the American Dream

T he idea of the American Dream is rooted in the United States Declaration of Independence, which proclaims that "all men are created equal" and that they are "endowed by their Creator with certain inalienable Rights" including "Life, Liberty and the pursuit of Happiness." In 1931, in the midst of the Great Depression, James Truslow Adams popularized the phrase "the American Dream" in his book, *The Epic of America*. He expanded on the original idea by saying that "life should be better and richer and fuller for everyone, with opportunity for each according to ability or achievement" regardless of social class or circumstances of birth. Today, the ethos has been simplified to mean that every American has the freedom to achieve prosperity — however he or she defines it.

I wrote this book for all the entrepreneurs who pursue their dreams of freedom. They symbolize all that is great about our country, and I respect and admire their courage. As a serial entrepreneur, I am one of the risk takers and feel compelled to share what I've learned with men and women who, with courage and determination, pursue the American Dream.

I have learned that the best of us embrace integrity. There are ruthless, unscrupulous individuals who achieve financial success, but they are in the minority; the only prosperity they know is financial prosperity. Men and women of honor and integrity create prosperity in many aspects of their businesses and their lives. They leave legacies that are greater than their inventories and balance sheets. They imbue values on their employees, customers, and business associates that reaffirm and validate the values that have made this country great.

It can be a hard and lonely road, though. It takes self-discipline and determination to persist when others would surrender. It takes faith when you need a "Yes," but so many say "No." Greatness is achieved when no one is looking; when there is no one there to support you in your struggle for the Dream. When doubt creeps in and it seems pointless to proceed, it takes discipline to make another call. And another, until, finally, you strike gold.

It begins with a simple transaction — a sale — and grows into a relationship. Our profession allows us to touch and influence many people in a unique and meaningful way. It can be a profoundly rewarding profession when we make the difficult or improbable happen with our discipline and integrity. We should take pride in what we do. As salespeople, we are part of an important "brotherhood"; defenders of free enterprise, exemplars of the American Dream.

Notes

Notes

_____

_____

_____

_____

_____

_____

_____

_____

_____

_____

_____

_____

_____

_____

_____

_____

_____

_____

_____

_____

_____

_____

_____

_____

_____

_____

_____